Equitation
For The Everyday
Rider

EQUITATION
for the Everyday Rider

LÉONIE MARSHALL

The Crowood Press

First published in 1996 by
The Crowood Press Ltd
Ramsbury, Marlborough
Wiltshire SN8 2HR

© Léonie Marshall 1996

All rights reserved. No part of this publication may be reproduced or transmitted in any form or by any means, electronic or mechanical, including photocopying, recording, or any information storage and retrieval system, without permission in writing from the publishers.

British Library Cataloguing-in-Publication Data

A catalogue record for this book is available from the British Library.

ISBN 1 85223 988 3

Picture Credits
All photographs by Vanessa Britton
Line-drawings by Rona Knowles

Typeset by Phoenix Typesetting, Ilkley, West Yorkshire
Printed and bound in Great Britain by WBC Book Manufacturers, Bridgend, Mid Glamorgan

CONTENTS

Introduction		6
1	Aims and Goals	7
2	Training Facilities and Yard Set-Up	24
3	The Principles of Training	37
4	Rider Position and the Aids	53
5	Lungeing and Long-Reining	67
6	The Horse's Paces	74
7	Straightness, Balance, Suppleness and Submission	84
8	School Movements and Exercises	94
9	Further Schooling on the Flat	104
10	Hacking Out	116
11	Gymnastic Jumping	123
12	Destinations and Objectives	135
Index		144

Introduction

Many people involved with horses nowadays are fortunate enough to have a good deal of tuition, and there is certainly plenty available to cater for every ambition. However, there are still a large number of aspiring riders who cannot afford lessons, and it is to these that this book is directed. Reading is an inexpensive form of finding out what you need to know; all that is needed then is plenty of hard work!

Another excellent way to learn is by watching others; you can see what is possible and how it is done. And you will have to try things out for yourself: experimenting is not wrong as long as the horse does not suffer, and it is often the only way to find out an answer. Try to develop a feel for what the horse is doing: this is the best way of all to find the truth – although it doesn't always work if a rider suffers from lack of sensitivity. It must be said that good feel is a gift and goes with an affinity with the horse in general, and those who lack this natural flair must work harder to find the way; nevertheless it is there for those who really look for it and are prepared to give the time to find it.

Equitation is based on two fundamental principles: first, the rider must learn to sit on the horse in such a way that he can give the aids clearly in a way that the horse will understand easily. Second, he must be prepared to devote sufficient time for the horse's mind and body to develop in such a way that the chosen goals are attainable.

These principles should be worked on daily if they are to become established; although this is no different to any sport where brain and muscle combine. Because each individual leads his own life there can be no set rules regarding routine, but everyone must have one if they are to be successful.

In the following pages riders will, I hope, find some suggestions as to how they may best help themselves and, as a result, help their horse as well.

CHAPTER 1
Aims and Goals

Before any aim or goal can be decided, the ability of both horse and rider should be assessed. If this is done sensibly, a good deal of disappointment might be avoided. It would, after all, be rather foolish even to consider competing at Badminton on a Shetland pony!

Assessing the Horse: Conformation

The skeletal structure of every horse is basically the same in respect of the bones it contains, but it is the way in which these are put together that makes the difference as to the horse's appearance and movement. It is important to appreciate this fact if a useful assessment of the animal is to be made.

Good conformation is more important for some disciplines than it is for others; for instance in showing it is essential, whereas in jumping it matters less. It can and does, however, affect performance. Moreover a horse with correct conformation can very often do more than one job in life because his build enables him to do so, whereas one with a fault is almost bound to be more limited. In an ideal world, one would look for the following good points:

- A pleasant head that matches the body.
- Large expressive eyes showing no white.
- Ears the right size for the head, preferably not lop.
- A well shaped mouth: not small or parrot-shaped.
- A full set of teeth in the adult horse, not worn or missing.
- A head set on to the neck with plenty of space for flexion.
- Good length of neck, rising strongly from the withers into an arch over the crest.
- A sloping shoulder.
- Withers prominent but not excessively.
- A back which is neither short nor long; well sprung ribs.
- Strong hindquarters with a good length of croup, and no obvious 'jumper's bump'.
- A tail joined to the hindquarters so that, when carried, it is an extension of them; low tails are unattractive.
- Limbs: look for a strong forearm and second thigh.
- Strong joints in proportion to the frame.
- Short cannons with plenty of width (bone), not 'tied in' (having proportionately insufficient diameter) below the knee joint.
- Firm pasterns of average slope.
- Round feet which are in propor-

AIMS AND GOALS

This horse is a little 'high behind', otherwise it seems a nicely proportioned animal.

tion to the horse; a strong wall to the hoof.
- A healthy underside to the hoof, in particular the frog.

The following points would be ones you might be advised to avoid:

- An ugly, heavy head.
- Very big ears.
- Small, mean eyes.
- Thickness where the head joins the neck.
- A 'ewe' neck, as this makes it very difficult for the horse to carry his head in the right position.
- An upright shoulder, because this often restricts the stride.
- A narrow frame, because it is often a sign of weakness.
- A long back can prevent the horse from engaging his hindquarters adequately.
- Weakness in the loin area can be a limiting factor in respect of the horse's propulsive power.
- Sloping hindquarters usually go with a low-set tail and probable lack of strength.
- A narrow forearm and second thigh lack support for the frame.
- Small, lumpy joints are less likely to be able to stand stress and strain.
- Long, very thin cannons may be too flimsy to stand very much.

AIMS AND GOALS

Assessing Temperament

Temperament is inherited, which is why it is so important not to breed from unsuitable animals. Each horse has his own personality, and owners should take the trouble to discover his type and individual character so as to be able to handle him in the most appropriate manner. Inappropriate or insensitive handling will almost certainly create problems which may never come right. Every horse will fall into a certain category, and these different categories need assessing in order to identify which one a horse belongs to, and thus be able to place him in a suitable sphere of equestrianism.

Highly Strung Horses

Horses that readily become anxious, tense or over-excited need sympathetic and knowledgeable handling. Becoming annoyed or impatient will usually make such animals worse, and generally the only way forwards with these is to be calm, quiet and self-disciplined yourself. The voice should be used in a soothing manner, and is then extremely beneficial, and the aids should be applied with the utmost sympathy.

Training may take time, and it is important to make allowance for this.

Lazy Horses

Idle horses which do not want to work tend to be stubborn, and unless they are shaken out of their lassitude early in their lives, they may well always try to avoid being energetic. Firm handling is essential, not only to alert their mind but to enforce physical response. Unfortunately inherent laziness can be

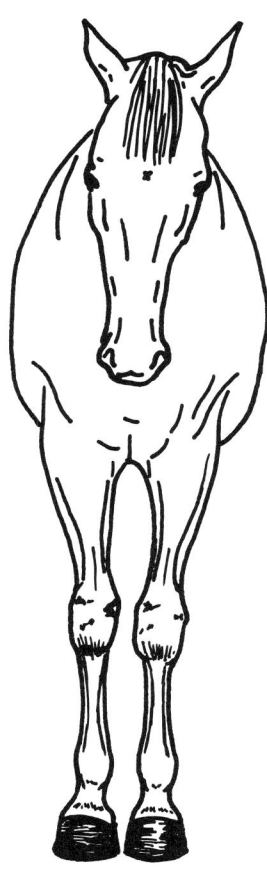

Horse narrow in front (knees almost touching).

- Excessively sloping pasterns: they can be vulnerable to wear.
- Upright pasterns can cause excessive jarring on joints.
- Small feet may hinder the bones of the foot.
- Flat feet are susceptible to bruising.
- Brittle hoof walls: because the wall breaks away readily the shoes tend to fall off.

AIMS AND GOALS

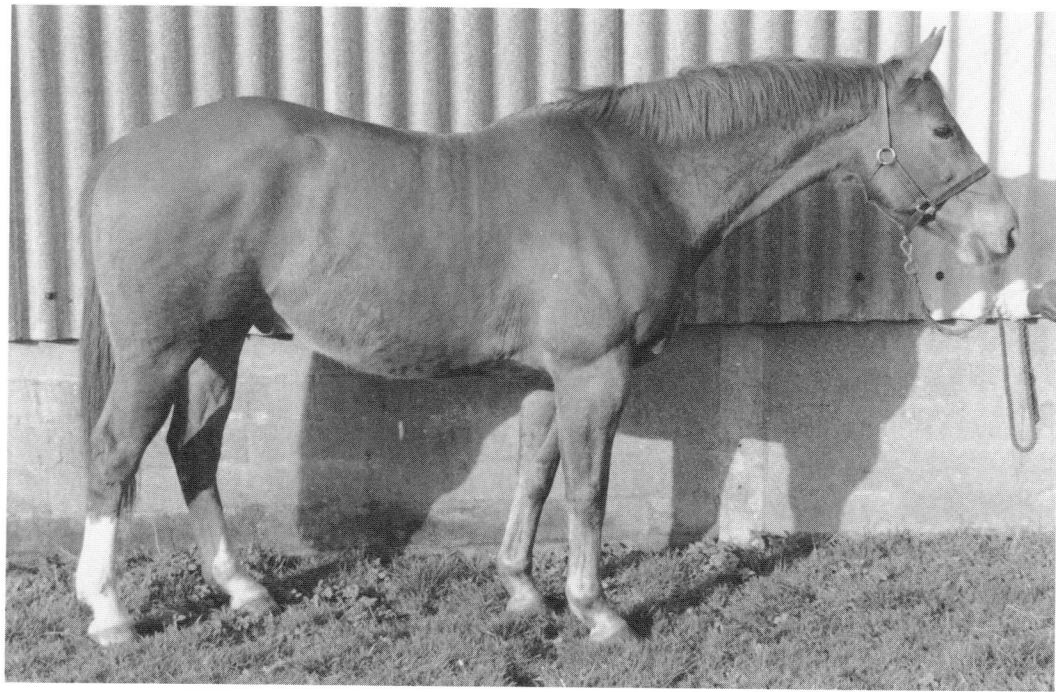

A heavier type of horse that could have better hindquarters but nevertheless looks a useful animal.

almost impossible to eradicate, and limits the horse's performance in many respects.

It can be hard work riding a lazy horse, which may even be fairly insensitive to whip and spurs. If it all becomes too much of a problem for you, it may be wiser to part company than to keep struggling towards a goal which, if you are honest about it, is probably unattainable.

Dull Horses

There are as many dull horses about as there are people, but this does not necessarily mean that they are unintelligent. Dullness may be induced by boredom, in which case more interesting or varied work will help. If an animal is genuinely slow-witted then a good deal of patient explanation is needed. Progress may be irritatingly slow, but many horses, once they have grasped what is wanted, retain the lesson well and become quite obliging.

An excessively dull horse may find his work just too much, and if he does, he may become stubborn about it and refuse even to try. In these circumstances it is probably futile to battle with him, and a less demanding career should be chosen.

Very Intelligent Horses

Any animal that is highly intelligent will have strong powers of learning, and – be quite clear about this – will be quick to pick up not only what is right but also

AIMS AND GOALS

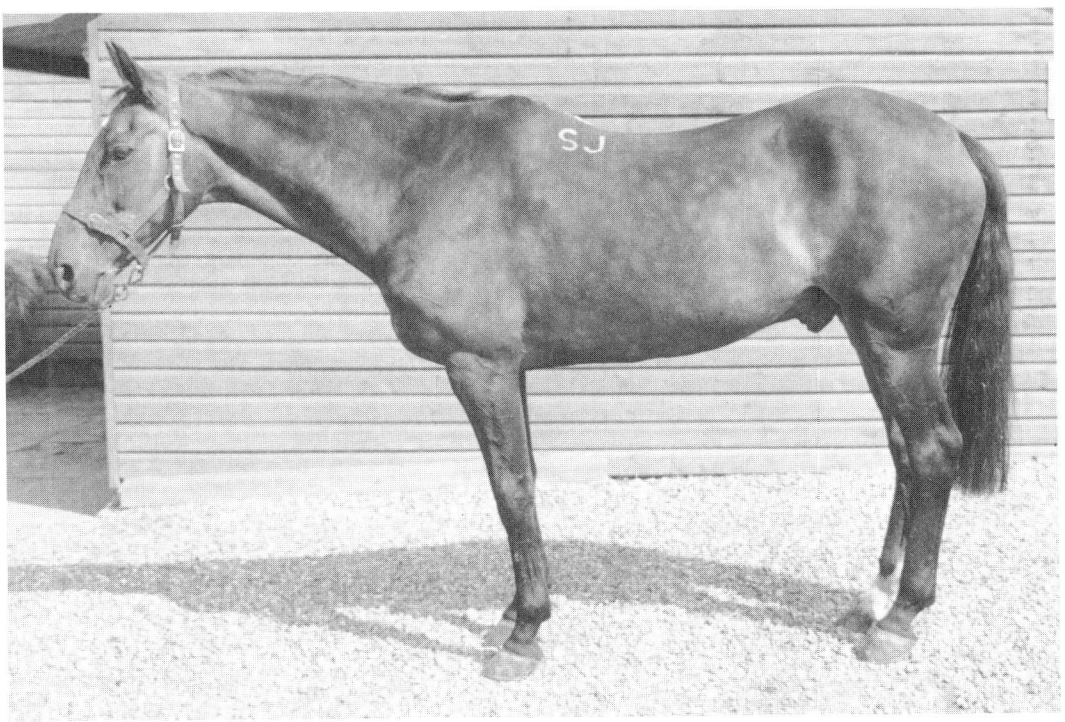

Quite a few faults can be seen in this picture. The head is slightly big. The back is long and slopes upwards to the croup which is short with a low set tail. The limbs are not 'set on' well to the body, making the horse stand on a short base.

what is wrong! He will be able to recall instantly any incident in his life, and his brain, because it functions so efficiently, will relay the messages it receives for motivation by the body at surprising speed. In fact his grasp of a learned exercise may be a handicap as he will be anticipating almost before he is asked anything by his rider. He will almost certainly have a strong sense of perception regarding his rider's physical and mental state, too.

Intelligent horses are a pleasure to teach as long as they are taught exactly. Make no mistake, any muddled thinking on the part of the rider may result in the horse deciding for himself, and if he happens to choose an answer whereby he succeeds in doing what *he* wants rather than what his rider is asking, this will be remembered and used again.

Nervous Horses

Nervous horses are worriers. They will often become anxious about objects or possible situations that are not there, as well as the ones that are. They may or may not be highly strung, but many are on edge about something they believe could,

AIMS AND GOALS

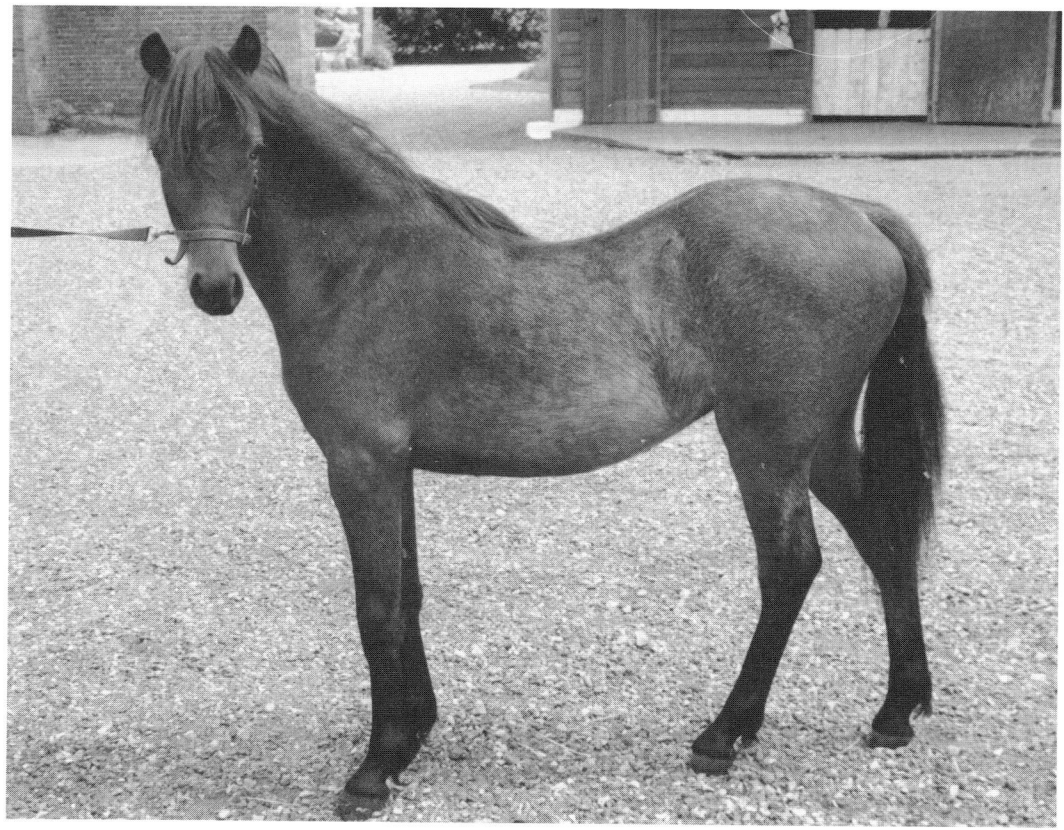

Youngsters are hard to assess but the rise to the loin seems excessive and the hing legs are very close together.

or is going to happen, and because they are anxious they often do foolish things that get them into trouble or hurt their owners. Often these horses develop a neurosis, especially if they have had a particular experience repeated, and once this happens only tolerance and patience can overcome the problems.

An owner must really like his horse if he is ever to help him gain in confidence, and there may be times when even this is not enough.

All nervous horses should be handled calmly and quietly. Sudden movements or loud noises will almost certainly startle them. If a horse panics, whether in the stable or being ridden, he is likely to be a danger to himself and to others, so the circumstances which have caused him to behave in this way should be avoided. Thus it is important to know what frightens the horse, so you can be sure he is never put in a similar situation again.

Nervousness in young horses often disappears as they experience more of life's vicissitudes, and become accustomed

AIMS AND GOALS

to all the things that heretofore they thought they were worried about. In an older horse it can be far more tiresome, and ones with genuine nerves may be unsuited to some work.

Aggressive Horses

An aggressive nature can be difficult to deal with; although most horses will, if firmly corrected, submit to their owner's wishes, there is always a minority which will not, and with these, correction can be virtually impossible if they have discovered that by using their aggression they can do what they want. This sort of animal will quite quickly develop an intimidating attitude, and once he has found that he can frighten his owner, he will not be easily subdued.

Aggression is an inborn defensive characteristic, and most horses will be aggressive in some degree towards their owners at some time in their lives. If this is dealt with immediately and in the right way, the horse will back off and not be aggressive again. The most effective form of punishment for unsociable behaviour is the whip, and it should be used at the time, and firmly enough that the horse feels it. Horses should not be hit more than a couple of times for each misdemeanour. Only in potentially dangerous situations should further punishment be necessary, when it is in everyone's best interest.

Some aggressive horses fight back, and with these the only real answer is to persevere until you win the battle, even if this seems an extreme course of action. Horses that are particularly nasty in the stable, or that kick out in response to the leg when ridden, should be dealt with very firmly indeed.

Being sure that the horse's temperament suits the work he has to do is important, but it is almost as vital that he is compatible with the person who is going to ride him. A person with an excitable, highly charged temperament is unlikely to get the best out of a nervous or highly strung horse, unless he or she is very knowledgeable. Similarly, a placid person may not suit a lazy horse.

Assessing Action

The way a horse moves will be a fairly clear indication as to whether he is suitable for the discipline in mind. Movement varies a good deal between different types of horse and inevitably one type will suit a certain job better than another. For instance a high, rounded action of the forelegs might suit a driving horse but would not be suitable for showing. The paces are described in Chapter 6 and it is essential that the owner understands what he should be seeing or feeling.

Whatever the breed or type, the hind legs should follow in the track of the forelegs. Sometimes they do not and this is undesirable whether it is due to a structural fault, muscular stiffness or simply as a result of bad riding. When seen from directly in front or behind, the horse should travel straight.

'Dishing' is when one or both forelegs swings out and to the side from the knee in the forward stride, and is quite common. It need not necessarily be detrimental for many purposes, although it would be for showing. Many people regard it as unattractive, but some of the world's highest winning horses have dished.

Pigeon toes, where one or both toes turn in towards the other, can also be unattractive, and furthermore this condition is

AIMS AND GOALS

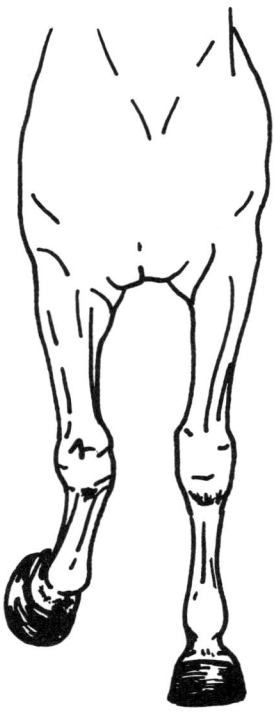

Dishing.

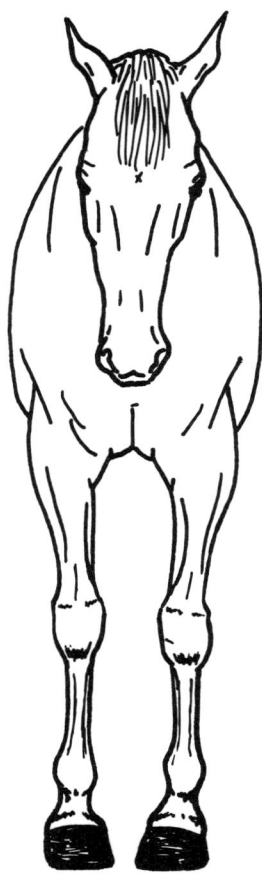

Pigeon toes.

more likely to affect performance because it can cause tripping. Pigeon-toed action is also likely to cause uneven wear on the bearing surface of the shoes which may become worn on one side only. This is particularly bad for the foot and associated joints, and may even cause subsequent lameness.

When assessing action, it is most important to view the horse from the side in order to judge the degree of driving power of the hind legs and their flexibility. Any unevenness of hock action or in the length of stride is a fault. The freedom and scope of the shoulders can also be best appreciated from the side; the shoulder should lift the foreleg so that it can reach upwards and forwards with ease and scope because in this way it can cover ground. This action should not be too exaggerated, and if it is, it is only acceptable if matched by the action of the hind legs.

In trot and canter there is a moment of suspension between each stride (see Chapter 6), and this is more pronounced in some horses than in others; a clear moment of suspension is an attribute.

AIMS AND GOALS

Back at the knee.

Over at the knee.

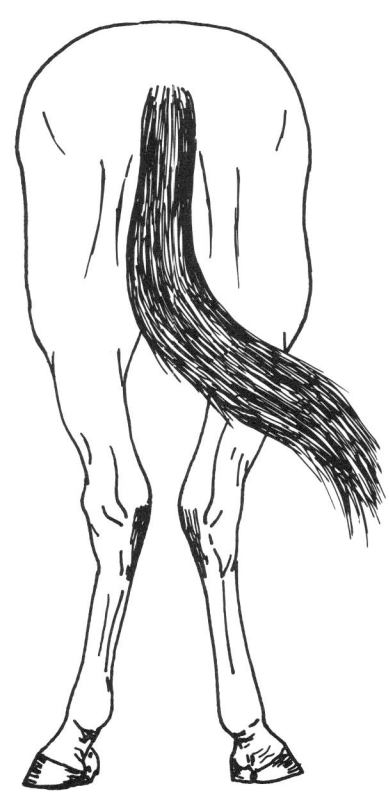

Cow hocks and turned-out toes.

Athletic Ability

A horse that is naturally flexible in his joints and supple in his body will find all forms of work easier than one that is not. However, the routine work he is asked to do daily should enhance and develop his gymnastic powers, and his mental learning should develop alongside his physical training so that he is able to respond when asked.

It is not merely the horse who needs to become an athlete: the rider should constantly train his own body and mind

AIMS AND GOALS

too, and make sure that he is fit for the discipline he wants to follow. Without the right sort of environment and programme of health and fitness this is not going to happen.

A rider must continually assess his horse's abilities so that he knows that whatever he asks of the horse is fair and possible. He must also learn to judge, if resistance occurs, whether it is because what he is asking is beyond the horse's capacity, or because he is being naughty; this is especially necessary when jumping. It is very distressing for the horse if he simply cannot accomplish what is being asked of him because of his physical limitations.

Assessing the Rider

Not only is it essential to form an opinion as to the horse's capabilities, it is also important to assess the rider.

Physique is important, and although a person can alter his or her physical appearance by diet or body building, his natural structure will always be an influencing factor. It is therefore only sensible to choose a discipline suitable for your body and characteristics. Of course, there are always exceptions and a person full of determination may overcome almost any disadvantage; people with disabilities have proved this frequently. Nevertheless your inherent character is bound to play a part, and for example those of timid disposition may just not be suitable for bold cross-country riding, however much they want to do this. Timid or nervous people also tend to infect their horse with the same tendencies, largely because they lack a positive attitude. Horses are extremely sensitive to fear, picking up signals which we inadvertently display. Any increase in our heart rate, breathing or body temperature will indicate itself to the horse, as will muscle tension.

Although most horses will not take advantage of a young child or a disabled person, they are generally quick to recognize weak, indecisive riding and will take advantage of it to get their own way. In similar vein, it might seem reasonable to expect that a confident rider would pass this feeling on to his horse, and indeed, combined with sensitivity and knowledge, this is indeed so. If, however, the rider is confident without due thought for his horse or his own actions, the way he carries on may lead to disaster. Many an accident occurs from over-confidence on the part of the rider which the horse does not share – and if he does, he is perhaps led into a situation that could hurt both himself and his rider.

A good rider is one who always considers his horse and blames himself.

Riding in a School Environment

Many people start their riding careers in a riding school, and a very good place to start this is, too, although it does have some disadvantages. Of necessity, however, riders generally find themselves in a group situation which limits their capacity to learn much about equitation; they are in fact there to be taught to sit on the horse properly and to learn basic control.

It is important to realize that there is a huge difference between this sort of activity, and riding one's own horse alone and independently. Many problems occur because riders fail to appreciate the difference between following round in a

AIMS AND GOALS

It can be fun to ride out with other horses and it is good for the horse's education.

ride, and being in a position of complete, unsupervised control. Horses are quite happy to follow each other, but they can be very reluctant when on their own. It is for this reason that new owners should be certain that they have reached a sufficient standard of proficiency to exercise adequate control over the horse, and that they fully understand the means of communication (see Chapter 4).

Riding at Home

All riders need certain qualities if they wish to be successful. First, they must be full of resolve to reach their chosen goal. Then they must be prepared to work exceedingly hard – only those with real dedication will achieve their objectives. They must combine patience and perseverance, and most importantly they must forge a sound partnership with their horse.

Always be prepared to learn and to listen to advice: some will be well founded, and some will be misguided, but watching the results of those that give it is a good guide. Follow the successful and discard the others. A lot will be gained by experience, by being out there and having a go; and as long as the right preparation is made and mistakes are rectified, progress will follow.

Some people are fortunate in having a natural feel: they undoubtedly have an advantage as they instinctively handle horses in the most appropriate and effective way. Not having this sort of 'feel' is a drawback, but it can be worked on and improved, and although it may take longer to make progress, these riders can in the long run be just as effective as anyone else.

Routine

Very little can be achieved without a planned programme of work and daily practice. Rider and horse need to develop together if ever they are to become in unison with each other, and only a progressive advance towards the chosen goal will establish this harmony. Each person will choose the routine which best suits him or her. Every sphere of riding requires variation, but for most disciplines, work in a school provides the best opportunity to lay down the fundamental principles: not only does it provide a suitable atmosphere for concentration, but the work done brings horse and rider closer together.

It will not matter to the horse if he is worked in the school and then goes for a

AIMS AND GOALS

relaxing hack, or vice versa. He may be schooled for only three days each week, have two days hacking or jumping and two days off; but whatever the work, it should be consistent. Only through continuity will the horse learn and improve.

Groundwork

All riding is based on rapport, the combined efforts of two individuals working as one, and this requires a great deal of understanding on the part of the rider. He must convey his wishes with tact if he is to expect his horse to trust him; and he must also understand how his messages are conveyed to the horse, and the sequence of events that goes on before the horse can reply (see Chapter 4). Moreover a knowledge of the horse's paces and the way in which he should work if he is to perform properly is essential (see Chapter 7); only if these points are observed will there be a suitable base upon which to build.

Aims and Objectives

Hacking is probably the least demanding form of riding and is a sphere of equestrianism that many people enjoy; it also has the advantage that almost any person or horse can take part. If pleasure is the rider's main reason for hacking, then in my opinion, the horses should also enjoy it – but unfortunately, they often do not. Thoughtlessly hammering along hard roads, or riding miles when the horse is unfit is not just unkind, it can also lead to lameness or ill health.

To gain full enjoyment, the rider should find out why the horse is happier when he is balanced, straight and so on (see Chapter 7); and he should ride with thought as to the effect his weight and aids are having. Thus a heavy rider who jabs his horse in the mouth or levers himself up by the reins is almost certainly doing a great deal of harm to his back and mouth.

In my view, it is just as important to school the horse even if you wish to do no more than go for an enjoyable hack, as it is for anything else, if only for the horse's sake (see Chapter 10).

Dressage

Competition work is very popular, but it is not easy to gain enough knowledge without quite a lot of help. There are riders who do manage adequately with very little tuition, but most people need critical appraisal every now and then.

It is possible to learn a great deal by going to competitions and watching other riders. Seeing the 'experts' working their horses in, and observing what they do in the arena is an invaluable experience.

Because dressage riding is an art, not many people can do it in the way it should be done. Many will go off and buy a trained horse and expect to get results just by pressing what they think are the right buttons. Horses certainly have good memories, and will retain established training remarkably well, but they cannot do so for ever. It is essential that the rider can feel what is happening underneath him if he is to be a successful dressage rider, and so those with some natural flair undoubtedly have the advantage.

Self-discipline is crucial to progress, and only those who feel that they are prepared to devote a great deal of time and effort to training should attempt this area of riding.

AIMS AND GOALS

It is also vital to have the right sort of horse because dressage is becoming increasingly competitive; to be successful nowadays at even a moderate level the horse must have exceptionally free and active action, he must look the part and his temperament must be suitable. Sometimes lesser horses will go quite a long way, but an animal which lacks scope in its action or is too idle by nature will generally not go far.

Showing

Much enjoyment and interest can be gained from showing, both in hand or under saddle; the purpose of this book, however, is to advise on the ridden aspect.

Those interested in showing will undoubtedly have decided in which area they are interested – hacks, hunters, cobs or Arabs – and are then in a position to purchase a horse suitable for that class; alternatively if they already own an animal, they must determine to which class it is best suited. Clearly the show horse or pony must have good conformation, and to be successful the best possible specimen of the type or breed is required. Inevitably judges vary as to the type they prefer, whether this is the lighter sort, or an animal of more substantial build; but owners who have shown for some time will soon discover which judges prefer what. It is wise then only to show under those who like what you have in order to avoid disappointment.

Good action is vital, and the first prerequisite is that the animal moves straight: that is to say, the hind legs should follow in the tracks of the forelegs, and there should be plenty of drive from the hind legs being placed under the horse's body; they should not be trailing out behind. The shoulders should lift the forelimbs to allow them the scope to reach forwards, but the action of the foreleg should be less rounded at the knee than for dressage.

A well mannered animal is essential because he must behave himself, not only in the company of others for the safety of all concerned, but he must also be safe for a judge to ride.

The rider should match the animal in height or build as far as possible. This is important to the picture they present and should not be dismissed as unimportant. A very fat person riding a small hack is unattractive, besides which he may well compromise the animal's ability to perform at his best.

Jumping

Those interested in any form of jumping must have the necessary courage: any negative thoughts or actions on the part of the rider will soon communicate themselves to their horse.

Horses of all types, shapes and sizes may prove to be good jumpers, so no rules can be laid down. The important thing is that a horse should want to jump, he should have the agility, and he should dislike hitting fences. There are many horses which will jump willingly but are careless, and this attitude may well be insurmountable: for show jumping this is, of course, no good at all, over cross-country fences it can be positively dangerous.

When assessing a horse's jumping ability it is not necessary to jump him over a big fence. It is often best to watch him jump loose in a school to see how he places himself and whether he bascules over the fence, tucking his legs up close to his body.

AIMS AND GOALS

Also in this way it is easy to observe his attitude, when rushing or undue hesitation may be an indication of possible problems.

Joining a Club

Joining a riding club is often a useful way to gain experience and receive extra help. Tuition from various experts in different disciplines is usually organized at a reasonable price, and there is always the social aspect, too! Most clubs take part in team competitions, and it can be fun to be included in these, providing as it does the opportunity to travel and the greater challenge of competing nationwide. Riding beneath a club's umbrella also provides a sound grounding for those with the ambition to further their knowledge in a particular area of riding.

Anyone can belong to a club on any type of horse, and there are events for people and horses of limited ambition or ability as well as for those who wish to go further.

Deciding your Goal

Each individual will differ as to how far he wishes to go with his riding, but a decision right from the outset will help to put him on a suitable road. Thus those with simple ambitions should not set themselves tasks which are unnecessarily difficult as this will only give them pointless frustration. Although every horse will benefit from basic school work, each rider must decide on his own commitment. If he wishes to compete in a simple dressage test, for instance, he must be prepared to do the work necessary, but he should not be put off by the idea that he needs to become a Grand Prix rider!

Those with higher ideals should determine what these are, but then should be patient enough to reach them by stages. An Olympic medal is only won by years of dedicated hard work, and is attainable by only a determined few. Nevertheless, having said that, I am all in favour of aiming at the top and getting as far as possible!

Tack

Every owner must be prepared to buy himself the appropriate equipment for his or her chosen discipline. As it is very expensive, due thought must be given before a choice is made.

For the horse, a snaffle bridle and well

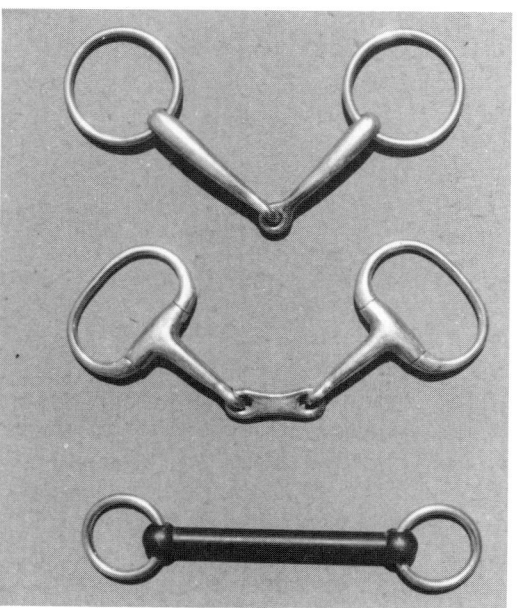

Three types of commonly used snaffle: at the top is a loose-ring Bridoon; the one in the centre is a French-link snaffle, a mild bit that many horses go well in; the bottom one is a vulcanite, straight-bar snaffle.

AIMS AND GOALS

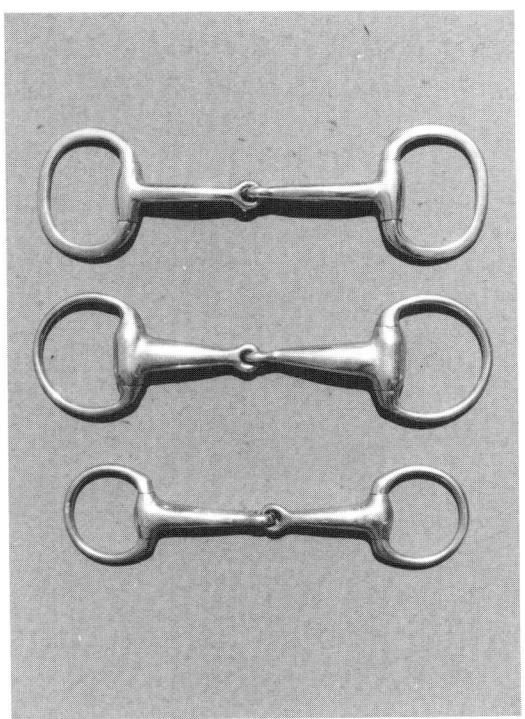

These are eggbutt snaffles, characterized by the fixed rings. All bits must be the correct width for the horse's mouth and not be too heavy. Many problems arise from insufficient thought on this matter.

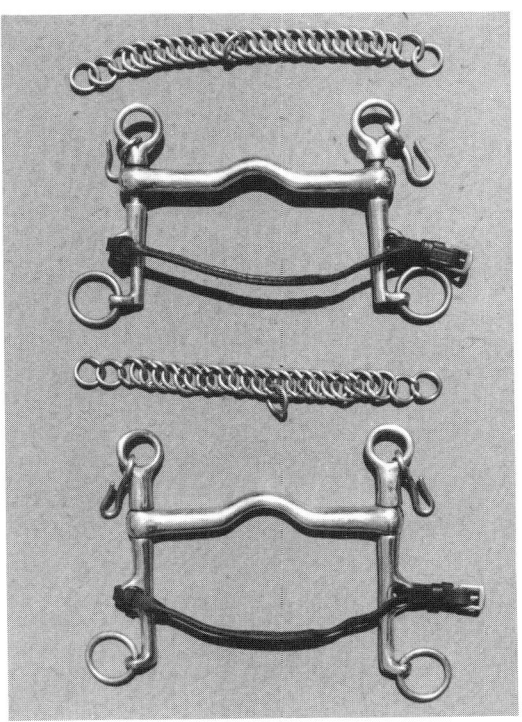

The curb part of a double bridle, which must not be used alone. The bottom one has longer cheekpieces, making the action of this bit more severe than the top one, which has a sliding mouthpiece. The ports on these bits are mild; higher ones may cause injuries to the roof of the horse's mouth. Curb-chains must lie flat, as shown, in the chin groove and should not be too loose.

fitting saddle is a basic requirement. Lungeing equipment may be necessary and clothing for travelling, and exercise boots are useful. The particular discipline chosen may demand extra articles of tack or clothing: a double bridle for showing, for example, and a show saddle; and when riding across country, a breastplate, a running martingale and a weight cloth may be required. It can be frustrating to be held back by not being dressed correctly or not having the right gear for the job, so it all needs to be planned.

The way to find out what is needed is to look up relevant rules or to watch other riders at appropriate competitions.

Progressive Training

Having determined his objective, each rider should then follow a progressive routine. He should begin with the basics and then progress by systematic

AIMS AND GOALS

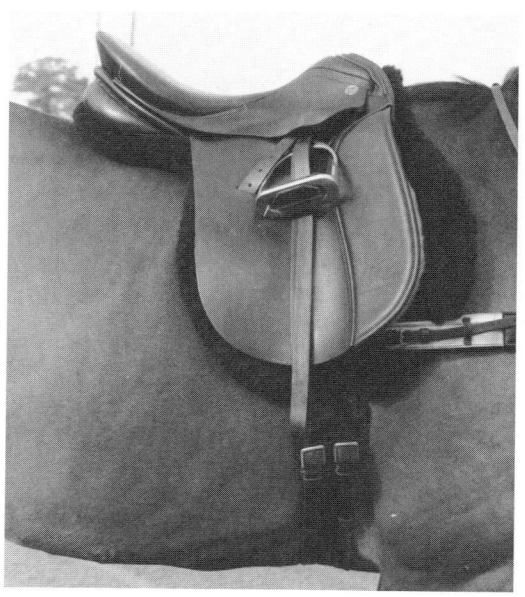

This dressage saddle looks as if it fits the horse and also shows how the shape of the seat will put the rider in a central position.

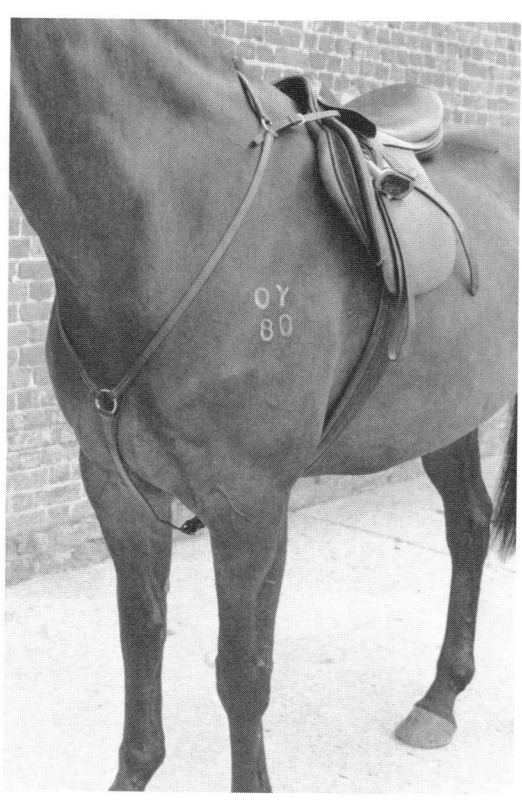

Breastplates are sometimes needed to help keep the saddle in place. This picture shows one correctly fitted. A slipping saddle is uncomfortable for horse and rider and is also unsafe.

This general-purpose saddle would throw the rider back making it impossible to sit correctly.

training, and clarity of thought, good planning and daily execution of this planning should produce the required development for both rider and horse. Remember, too, that a strict stable routine is just as important to the horse as his ridden training, because only if he is healthy and fit can he perform properly.

Watching experts in the chosen field of riding is a tremendous help for any aspiring competitor; observing their techniques and what they expect from their

AIMS AND GOALS

This double bridle looks to be a good fit and the horse is happy in his mouth.

horse, and noticing the 'tricks of the trade', are all invaluable pointers to progress. It may be possible to arrange professional help from someone who is clearly at the top of a particular sphere – although a word of warning here: not every instructor will suit every pupil, and it is important that there is a rapport. And just because a rider does not get on with a particular teacher does not mean that he is a failure: with another teacher he may do well.

Perhaps one of the most important aspects of riding is the capacity to feel what is going on, and it is essential that the rider learns this in each new exercise he tackles.

CHAPTER 2
Training Facilities and Yard Set-Up

Given unlimited finance it would not be a problem to organize the ideal facilities for training. A purpose-built stable yard, outdoor and indoor riding areas, a flat paddock for jumping, undulating land upon which to build cross-country fences and post-and-railed paddocks for turnout would be everybody's dream. In reality, of course, many horse owners are forced to compromise and, as with all compromises, it is not always easy to decide on the priority. If riding is of first importance then a schooling area is essential. However, before going into this in more

The horse will not work well if he is not properly fed and cared for. A horse in good condition, who is then well-turned out, is a pleasure to work with, enhancing your positive feelings towards him.

TRAINING FACILITIES AND YARD SET-UP

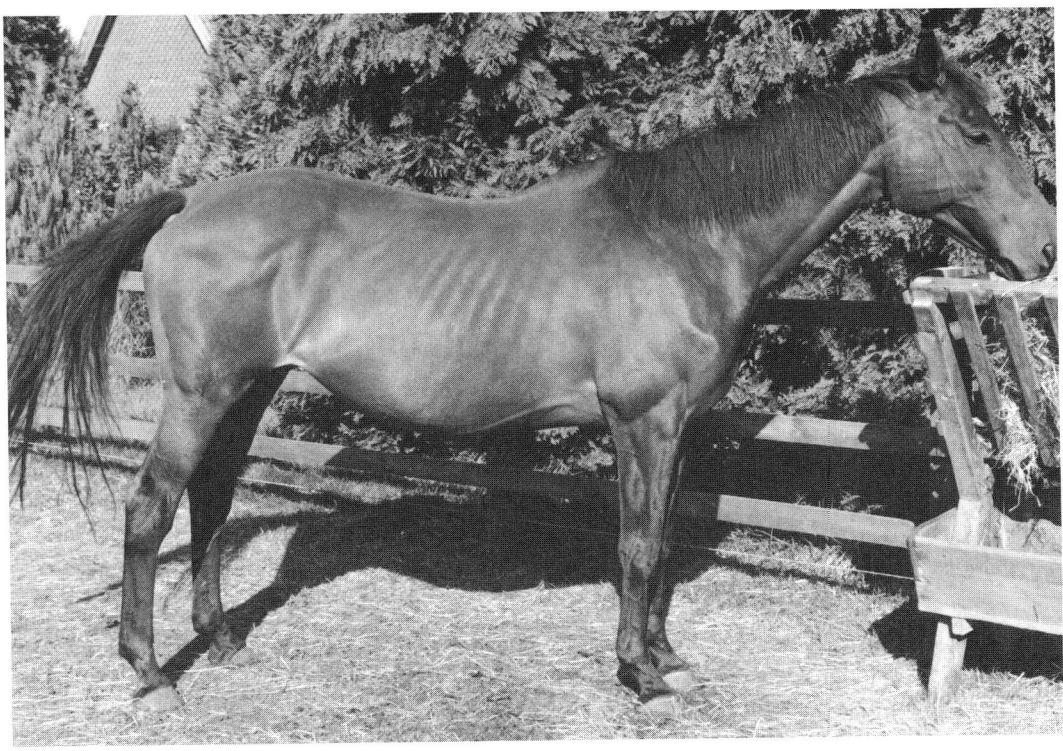

Although this horse's coat is shiny, he has no muscle and he is very lean.

detail I would like to stress how vital it is to house the horse suitably, and to have a place where you can turn him out so he can let off steam.

Health and Well-Being

Good health is essential to successful performance. First, it is an owner's responsibility to ensure that the stable provided gives the horse maximum comfort and freedom to move around. Mentally he will be relaxed in this environment, and he will then be more receptive when ridden. Free access to water, and a sensibly planned diet for his age, size, temperament and work programme will help him physically so that he can put in the effort that will be required of him.

On a limited budget a purpose-built yard may be an impossibility, but horses have proved to be perfectly happy in many different types of building as long as they have space, air and light, and preferably a view; they like nothing better than to be able to observe their owner's goings-on, and this association does aid in the building of a rapport. In my opinion it is most important that the horse should be happy, as he is then far more likely to cooperate than he would if he were miserable. It is difficult enough training a

TRAINING FACILITIES AND YARD SET-UP

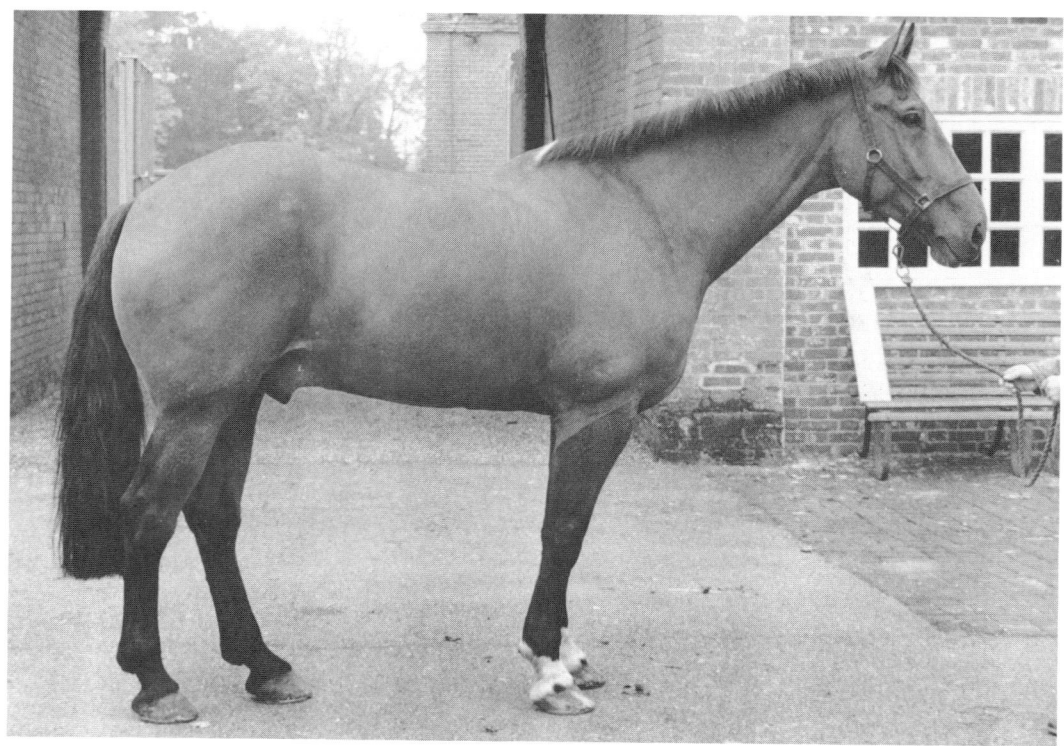

This horse looks well. He is stabled and is in work, so he has been given a hunter clip to save him from losing condition from sweating when he is worked.

horse to do what is wanted anyway, without having to contend with active opposition or sullenness.

Having the freedom to express himself is the status quo for the horse in his natural state, and is an instinctive outlet, and he should have the chance to follow his own inclinations either in an enclosed safe arena or in a well fenced paddock. Most horses that are kept stabled in fact quite like the safety of their loose-box and the constant supply of food, and so they are generally happy to return to it, once they have had a roll or a gallop round. Owners may worry about injury during this sort of exercise, but you can always put on protective boots.

The Training Areas for Flatwork

It is essential that the horse is in a receptive frame of mind if he is to learn anything at all. Pent up by overfeeding or lack of work he will be frustrated and unable to concentrate, so his nutrition and exercise should be constantly monitored.

The next crucial matter is to have somewhere to ride where there are the least number of distractions – and it is not only to the horse that this applies! If the rider's concentration is interrupted by watching his dogs playing or his children getting into mischief, there will be little

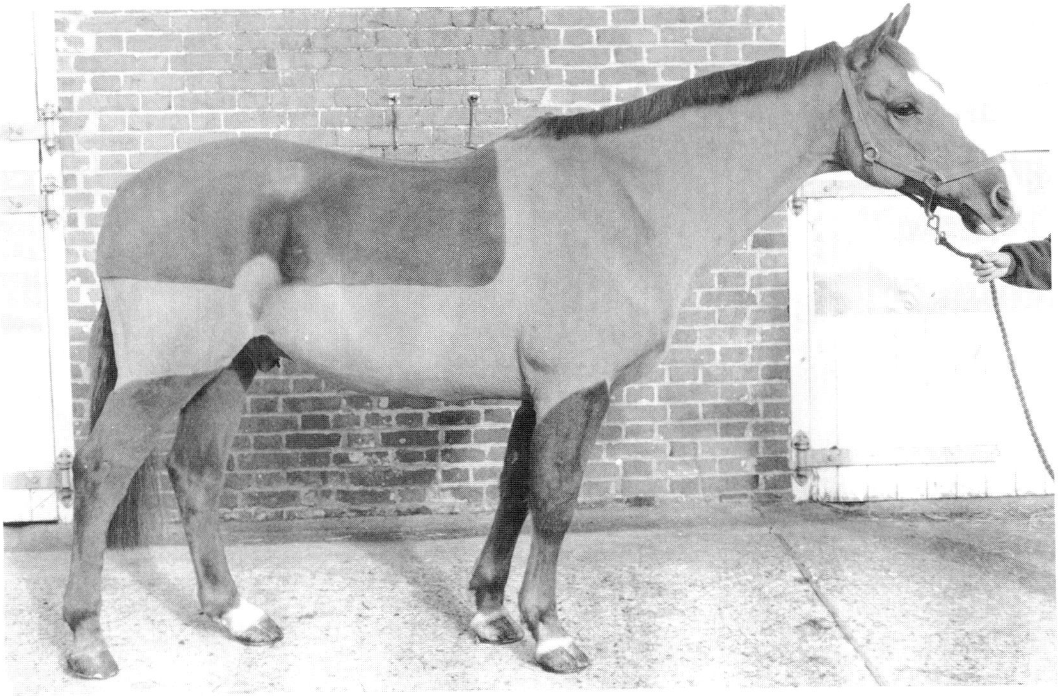

TRAINING FACILITIES AND YARD SET-UP

A blanket clip is an alternative type of clip very often used when the horse is in only moderate work.

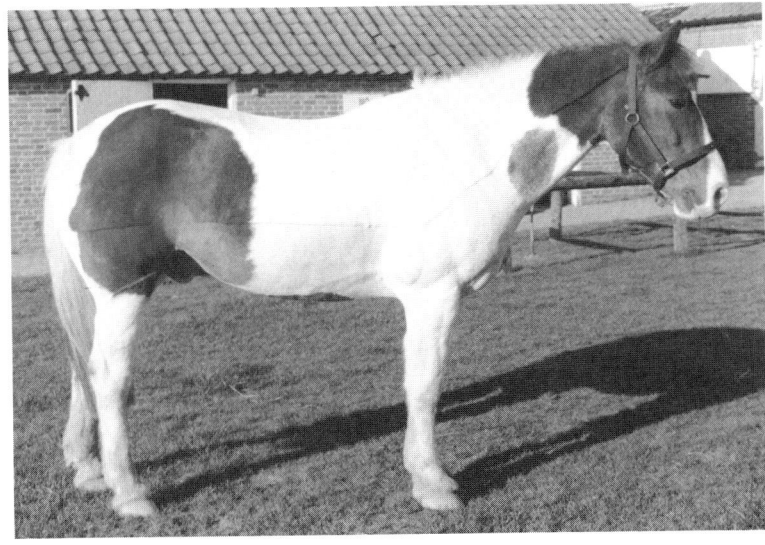

If the horse has to spend time in the field as well as having to work, a trace clip is a good compromise since it provides some warmth.

TRAINING FACILITIES AND YARD SET-UP

In winter, or if the horse is clipped, he must be kept warm. The cross-over rug shown above is a very good type to use as it is quite secure and unlikely to slip. When turned out for exercise or to graze in winter, the horse should wear a New Zealand rug (below).

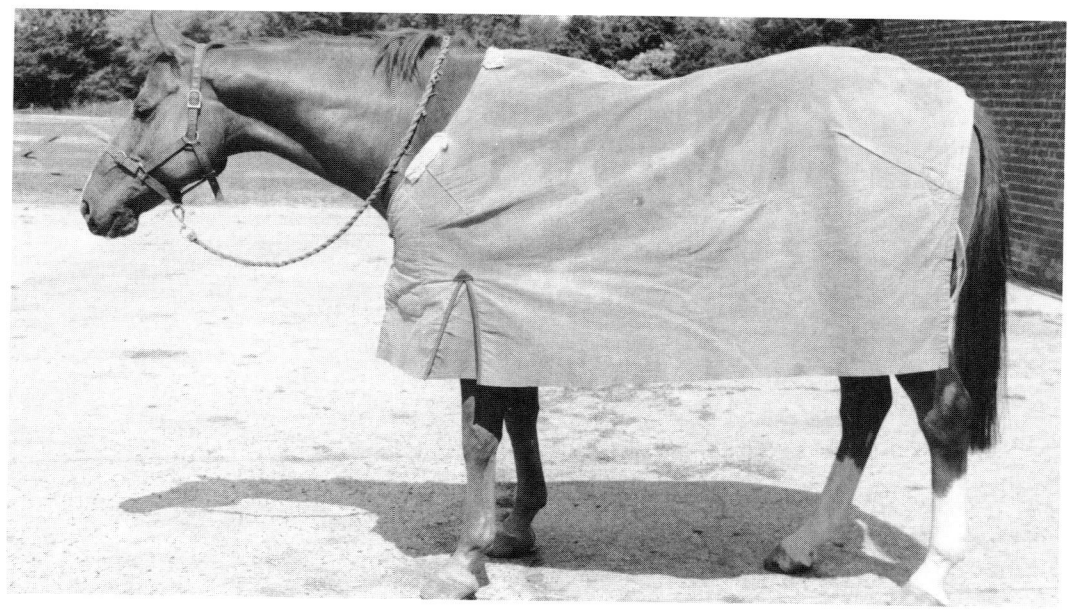

TRAINING FACILITIES AND YARD SET-UP

work done. As far as the horse is concerned, it is better if he cannot see his friends or other animals in the neighbouring field. A quiet area properly marked out is needed if the job is to be done well.

Not everyone is fortunate enough to have an all-weather surface. Some people have to ride in a field, and if this is the case the going is important. It may not be possible to use the same area all the time as it will become too cut up, so it is useful to have cones or markers which can be moved around easily. Also, it is a good thing to train the eye to assess the area required for schooling, so that markers are not necessarily needed at all. For many years I trained in the middle of an open field, and although this is not satisfactory as a permanent arrangement, it does mean that work can go on.

One of the handicaps of a field is that in the winter it generally becomes muddy and slippery, and this can dramatically hinder the regularity and rhythm of the horse's paces. For those who do find themselves in this situation, however, I would nevertheless encourage them not to despair, because there are still some grass verges left or woodland clearings that suffice until the weather improves! Failing that, quite a lot can be achieved on the roads (see Chapter 10).

For the serious student with high ambitions, a proper arena is ultimately desirable – but even this need not be all that expensive. We have had very satisfactory arenas consisting of a chalk base

The right environment is essential. This outdoor school is well fenced and the surrounding trees and upward slope of the land around the school offer protection from the weather.

TRAINING FACILITIES AND YARD SET-UP

An indoor school is invaluable during the winter months, and when learning to ride or for breaking young horses, as it is safe and the surface is consistent.

covered with a thin layer of sand (about 2 in); they are weather-proof and safe to work on. We have also used river stones as a base, graded into layers ranging from quite large lumps of rock to small flat pebbles; once rolled, this forms a solid foundation upon which sand or other material can be laid.

The surface must be surrounded with supporting sleepers or planks to stop it spreading, and having it fenced is also an advantage. Most horses will attend to their rider better if they know they are contained.

As far as surfaces are concerned, there is so much choice nowadays that what is chosen is entirely up to the individual preference and depth of pocket. What is of most importance is that it is satisfactory to work on, and that it is of non-slip material is essential because if the horse slides he may not only lose confidence but could injure himself as well. Too hard a surface or one where stones are likely to bruise the foot is plainly a mistake, but equally the horse will not appreciate floundering through deep going; this is both exhausting and dispiriting for him.

One of the chief hazards of riding outside is, of course, the weather. Nevertheless every rider has to learn to cope with excessive heat, teeming rain or even gales; and although horses are often affected by the weather, they have to learn to be disciplined in spite of it. However, although this is all a necessary part of training, to ride in a sheltered place is more desirable, and much more conducive to productive work. On the whole we have found trees to be the most useful form of protection, and have planted the fast-growing *Leylandii* round the edge of our schools.

Indoor Schools

Those fortunate enough to have indoor facilities do have a great advantage, but it must be said that they are not the be-all and end-all; and indeed, it is essential that you train outside as well. Many is the time when I have come up against terrible conditions at a show and have been thankful that I have persevered against the elements when training at home. Indoor work is most useful in that the surface is not variable and provides the best possible chance to regulate the paces; the horse can feel confidently foot-sure, and the rider can devote his attention towards precision.

Young horses benefit from being able to concentrate on their work, and the indoor school offers a secure environment for rider and horse to get to know each other. In winter it means that work can carry on, an eventuality which provides continuity and so a better chance to progress.

One disadvantage is that indoor surfaces do need to be kept damp. Dust is a hazard to health and should be avoided, so constant watering is necessary.

The Training Area for Jumping

Showjumping

Ideally the best place to teach the horse to jump is on an all-weather surface, first

It is essential to school your horse in a place that is free from distractions. This horse and rider are clearly concentrating on each other.

and foremost because it offers protection against jarring which so often causes lameness. The surface should be firm, with no likelihood of the horse skidding should he stop sharply or if he becomes unbalanced. Loss of confidence from this cause is common, but it is not always recognized as a hazard by owners. Stripped bark is often unsuitable for jumping for this reason.

An ordinary-sized dressage arena (40 × 20m) may be used, but this becomes restricting after a while, and most people who jump prefer an area of at least 60 ×

TRAINING FACILITIES AND YARD SET-UP

40m. This may, of course, be impractical for the majority of people who probably count themselves lucky if they possess a reasonably flat paddock! Personally I prefer one that is not too large, and is well fenced; this is more conducive to concentration, and is safer if the animal becomes strong. A stout gate is advisable, which should be kept closed during training. This will deter most horses from returning to the stable yard in a moment of antagonism, although I did once find myself involuntarily clearing it instead!

If the jumps are moved frequently, the ground should not become too poached; this may be rather an effort, but it is important. Slippery take-offs inevitably cause trouble, and jumping out of deep mud is a bad idea anyway.

Some owners fail to realize that the ground can be almost as slippery when it is hard and dry as when it is wet, especially if there is no 'top' on it. When training a youngster it is so important to maintain his confidence that every point should be considered, and the going is of as much significance as the fences themselves.

Basic schooling over fences is explained in Chapter 11, but for those who may be anxious that they cannot afford proper jumps, let me reassure them that much can be achieved with a couple of poles and two oil drums!

Cross-Country Jumping

A pre-requisite for cross-country schooling is undulating ground so that fences can be placed in a variety of positions on the slopes. Needless to say, not everyone is that fortunate, but a lot of preparatory work can be done for example out hacking, when there may be quite a few opportunities to practise over small obstacles; and the horse can at least learn to use himself effectively up and down hills.

Hacking

Most riders enjoy hacking their horse, or they may even do so for specific reasons (see Chapter 10). However, not everyone lives in an area where it is safe to ride out, so many will box up their horses and take them to places that are more suitable. It is my belief that hacking is beneficial to horse and rider and should be part of the training programme – but a word of caution: novice riders, or riders with young horses are advised to go out in company; and you should never jump when out alone, however tempting it may be.

Jump-Building

Although it is an advantage to have a set of showjumps and a cross-country course this is not always possible; and although buying jumps is an expensive business, the ingenious DIY can be just as good. Of course, it is very important to know how to bolt one piece of wood to another safely, as a 15cm (6in) nail can be exceedingly dangerous!

Poles should measure 10cm (4in) in diameter, and wings should stand securely and have blunt-ended holders for the poles. When not in use, all jumps should be stored in a safe place.

Cavaletti are very useful indeed for the early training of both horse and rider, although it must be stressed that they should not be stacked. Their use is explained in much more detail in Chapter 11. A variety of coloured poles and planks, a wall, gate, and brush fillers are also

TRAINING FACILITIES AND YARD SET-UP

Building small versions of cross-country fences to practise over at home is essential if the intention is to go horse trialing. Strongly built, secure, and inviting fences such as this will be safe to jump.

worth having. They can all be made or painted at relatively low cost.

Cross-country fences can be built round the edge of a field or paddock using any available piece of undulating ground. Anyway, since the horse's early training is more to do with practising maintaining pace and being able to keep control, rather than jumping a large variety of fences, it hardly matters if the course is somewhat restricted. Nevertheless a young horse does need to see different types of obstacles, and this can be achieved by building small replicas of fences seen at competitions. A water jump is less easy to manufacture, but is undoubtedly useful if you can contrive something. To teach your horse to jump into water, it may be necessary to take him to where there is a shallow stream or river in order to practise. It is absolutely essential that this has a solid bottom, as many accidents occur through the ground giving way.

For those who need to gallop their horse as part of a fitness programme, a local farmer may be willing to allow use of a field, or it may be necessary to look elsewhere. A beach, if available, is ideal for this purpose.

TRAINING FACILITIES AND YARD SET-UP

Going to a show will give you an insight into the sort of fences needed for training.

Sometimes it is necessary to recreate a 'bogey' fence. Letters on fences or strange wings and pots of flowers can be objects to be overcome.

TRAINING FACILITIES AND YARD SET-UP

Keeping the Horse at Livery

Not everybody can afford the kind of facilities that are required to train their horse at home. Some may prefer, or may be obliged, to keep their horse at livery where someone else sees to its everyday needs, and where there are opportunities which would not otherwise be available. In this sort of set-up there is usually someone at hand who, even if he or she cannot provide instruction, will offer advice if needed.

Another advantage is that there will always be company for the horse who, like most species, likes to have another of his own kind in close proximity. Horses which live together are generally more relaxed, they eat better and so come to their work in a better frame of mind. There can, however, be problems if one takes a particular liking to another, and does not wish to be separated from it when taken out for its training; but learning to work on its own is all part of its development – so it probably does no harm, either.

Working in company is also useful: it teaches the horse to go beside another, to pass or go away from others, and to learn to concentrate on his rider rather than being distracted by his friends. If he is nervous of something there is usually an older horse to give him a lead.

At a riding school or livery yard there is always something going on, which is good experience for the horse and may benefit the rider also.

The disadvantage to the serious student is such that because there are a number of people about and a great deal of general activity, it may be hard to find a place to work quietly. Moreover, any frustration on the part of the rider will be felt by the horse and may affect his response. It is not necessary or sensible to work the horse either in company or alone all the time, but most people concentrate better by themselves and this should be borne in mind, especially when attempting to teach something new.

Even if the choice of livery yard is limited, it is advisable to inspect the place before making a commitment. It can be very annoying to find your horse's health is jeopardized because you have placed it with people who lack the knowledge to care for it properly.

The ridden horse will normally require clipping in the winter months so that he does not lose condition from excess sweating due to his training. Yet another advantage to having him at livery is that in a professional yard this facility will be available. And if competitions are the aim, there may be the chance to share transport for those unable to provide their own. All these details should be considered, because they will affect the horse's training and its result.

The Horse Kept on its Own

Training a horse entirely on its own has the advantage of the rider being able to establish the closest possible rapport with it, and the best chance of gaining its fullest attention. However, although being in a quiet place where maximum concentration is possible is ideal for some of the time, such isolation is not practical for ever and the horse must be brought into different environments; part of his training should expose him to situations that cause him to become excited or inattentive. Only by doing this can the rider hope to overcome any problems.

TRAINING FACILITIES AND YARD SET-UP

Horses are distracted or excited by so many things, and their attention can be claimed in a second, long before their rider is aware of anything else; so when planning a horse's future, he can be prepared for the experiences it might bring in certain practical ways. For instance, the trainer should think about creating various hazards in order to accustom the horse to them and thereby reduce his alarm; with a little ingenuity, an owner can arrange for the horse to see or hear many of the things he will eventually come across at some time in his life. Perhaps a genuine loud-speaker, or a strange-looking person selling multi-coloured balloons would be rather difficult to arrange, but a tape recorder or a variety of odd objects tied to a fence or draped over a gate will give a horse the chance to develop confidence in his rider and overcome fears. By the same token, the rider will find out how his horse reacts, what he is most alarmed by, and what he takes in his stride. This kind of mutual discovery is very important to future progress.

There are many problems which arise when training horses, and having unsatisfactory facilities can be a barrier that may seem insurmountable. I do know from experience, however, that if a rider has the will, there is nothing at all that will prevent him or her from proceeding.

CHAPTER 3

The Principles of Training

Any successful rider who claims to be entirely self-taught is indeed remarkable and must be very gifted. Most people need teaching either on a regular basis or at frequent intervals, with 'homework' being given to work on. Instruction is expensive, and it may not be easy to determine the quality. Qualifications should be an indication but are not always, and trying to differentiate between the really good teacher and the one who only thinks he is can sometimes be perplexing.

This book is primarily for those riders with a limited purse who necessarily must help themselves; however, one of the chief methods of learning is by listening to others, and therefore I intend to try to give some guidance on this subject.

How the Rider Learns

Instruction

Instruction is available in a variety of ways. The riding school is the obvious one to start, but as already mentioned, there are very few which teach more than the basics and although this may be useful in the beginning, the more ambitious rider will soon outgrow that level. Club rallies or organized shared lessons are the next possible choice, and this sort of group instruction can certainly be most helpful up to a point. Sharing a lesson with some like-minded person is yet another possibility, although you might find that if you do so for any length of time, the horses will need to work at different exercises due to their age or ability, or one rider will progress more quickly, giving the other an inferiority complex!

In short, individual instruction is the only meaningful way to proceed. With this one-to-one method, the finer details can be discussed and your particular problems sorted out as they arise.

Finding a suitable teacher in your locality may be difficult, but to go to a teacher just because he or she is the nearest is certainly not the best solution. Thus travel may be inevitable, although to the keen rider this should not be too much of a problem; at one period in my riding career I was only able to see my trainer for five days twice a year, but this did not stop me from making significant progress! Nowadays many freelance teachers will travel to their pupils, and this may be a solution for those riders with limited time.

Deciding who you have to teach you depends, in my opinion, on whether they have proved themselves in competition in your chosen sphere. Thus it would be better to spend your hard-earned money on a few lessons with someone of repute, than to have a great deal of help from a person with less knowledge. Also it is important to have a certain empathy with the teacher. Even instructors of the

THE PRINCIPLES OF TRAINING

highest calibre are clearly not really interested in some of the people they teach, and if they are not prepared to make the effort, their pupils will not gain anything from them. Before making any commitment to take regular tuition it is wise to have just one lesson to start with, so as to assess an instructor's input and interest in you.

A sympathetic teacher is a lifeline and should be treated with respect. He has got where he is by years of hard work, and he will not, for example, appreciate being kept waiting, nor being telephoned at ten o'clock at night to be given a detailed account of how the horse performed in his last novice class! On the other hand, I am bound to say that many teachers will willingly give advice out of hours to pupils with whom they have been associated for some time and who are doing well.

As a teacher myself, however, I would like to make the point that it is hard to be patient with riders who try to monopolize your time, or with those who always blame their horse!

Having decided on the time and finance available and having chosen a teacher, the rider should now seek additional ways to increase his knowledge. Even if he only has a lesson four times a year, what he learns during that time he will undoubtedly put to good use; but this must be backed up by other methods.

Study

Reading is one relatively cheap way to learn more about a chosen subject, and there are plenty of books available from shops or book clubs. Some people will find this form of learning appealing; others, however, may find it hard work, and my advice to these would be to read up about some particular exercise, then go and try to ride it, and then come back and read about it again! Nevertheless, books can be daunting unless directly associated with the practical aspect, and as so much of successful riding is to do with feel, the intellectual side is bound sometimes to take second place.

Having a video made is an excellent way to study performance, either one's own or that of someone more expert, although much depends on the quality of the film as blurring may distort significant details. The important thing when watching your own performance is to be self-critical, not to the point of becoming totally disillusioned but certainly trying to be honest. Everyone believes their own horse to be the best, but a sensible appraisal is needed if improvement is to be made.

Watching

A tremendous amount can be learned by watching others ride, and those you observe don't even need to be expert — although of course it is essential to study the right way of doing things as well as noticing how not to do it! The really important point to remember is not to watch critically or superficially but to keep an open mind. At shows, one rider can often be heard condemning another, but he or she is not really looking to see what is going on. Sometimes the reason for a particular way of riding is not apparent at first, but by watching carefully you come to appreciate its purpose.

Seeing the experts work their horses prior to a class at a show can be fascinating and of great value. How they apply the aids and what they expect of their horses may come as a surprise, and can certainly provoke further thought; not

THE PRINCIPLES OF TRAINING

only does it provide an insight into a deeper knowledge, it may also give a clue as to the expected outcome.

Watching riders who obviously have less experience, or even very little knowledge at all, is also useful because their horses will clearly be struggling to work out what is wanted and finding it very hard to carry out. By way of comparison, it should be evident that the expert makes riding look easy, while the lesser rider makes it all look very difficult indeed!

Experiment

When working alone, a certain amount of self-discovery is essential; moreover if you didn't experiment, you wouldn't learn very much. Although riders should take care that their horses are not caused to suffer as a result of what they ask them to do, a process of trial and error is bound to take place to some degree. It takes a little courage sometimes to venture into an unknown area, but it is also exciting and stimulating. After all, progress is only achieved by sorties into new territory, and as long as this is done with some planning, not too much harm will be done.

Because training is all about a *gradual* development of mind and muscle, every rider should remember that each new exercise should build upon the one before; in this way fewer mistakes will be made. Failure to follow this logical approach would be rather like trying to learn advanced mathematics before being able to count. The fundamental principles are explained in later chapters, but it is important to appreciate that without them as a basis, no experiments can be made at any stage. Thus the rider's seat and aids, and the horse's basic paces are the bedrock: establish these soundly in the first instance, and many fascinating openings will then lie ahead.

Before you experiment – such as training the horse to do flying changes, or asking him to jump a type of fence he has not seen before – it is just as well to seek advice; but if it is not possible to have practical help, then you must use your head and work it out for yourself!

Going to a Show

One useful way of learning is by competing; in fact, going to competitions is an essential part of training. At home it is easy to be deluded into thinking that everything is perfect, and often it is only by comparison with others that a realistic assessment of your own standard can be made.

A show is a good education for the horse, too, a place where many new things can be discovered. Furthermore the experience may bring to light some aspect of your riding you had not previously thought about: other riders or judges may make comments that are enlightening, and sometimes even ordinary spectators do this! A rider will learn a great deal about his own horse, too: about his mental attitude to different situations, and how he handles himself physically when under pressure. He will also find out about himself, where his weaknesses lie, and aspects of performance which must be worked on more seriously.

Ring nerves can be a big handicap and have to be overcome: the psychological problem of not allowing other competitors or a nerve-racking situation to affect the way one rides needs some conquering, and facing up to disappointment cheerfully can be a hard lesson to learn.

THE PRINCIPLES OF TRAINING

Success, on the other hand, is heady, but equally it must be put into perspective. To have won an Olympic medal may be an excuse to be proud, but having won the local open jumping is not necessarily a reason to boast! Success and failure walk hand in hand, and as such should be accepted as part of learning. As long as a rider has this attitude he should never feel irrevocably dismal, nor should he consider himself above others, but he will continue to explore new ground with enthusiasm. The marvellous thing about horses is that the subject is endless!

The Process of Learning for the Rider

It is important to understand exactly what goes on in our *own* minds so that we can better understand our horses. We learn largely by way of the senses, through which we see, hear, touch, smell or taste the things around us – as does the horse. Unlike the horse, however, humans have the advantage of speech, by which faculty one human can communicate his knowledge to another. This is tremendously important, as it goes a long way towards avoiding confusion. Also, because the human being is a logical thinker, he is able to reason out points for himself.

For most human beings in everyday life, the coordination of mind and limb presents no difficulty. However, when placed in close relativity to the activities of an animal, certain problems may arise. Thus a rider on a trained horse may, if he is taught, be able to make that animal perform almost as well as its trainer; but given an untrained animal, the situation can be entirely different. A horse left to his own devices will react instinctively to each situation he finds himself in; the rider who is unaware of this fact may be caught out, and may find his own reactions differ to the horse's, or become uncoordinated: instead of working together, mind and limbs may be momentarily disrupted, and the result will be muddled. It is plain therefore that the rider should know exactly where he wants to go and at what speed, and that he knows how to indicate this to the horse and is able to do so clearly via the aids.

Without clear thought, the mind cannot transmit your intentions to the body in a logical way, in which case the limbs will not move with clear definition, either.

Concentration

The ability of the rider to focus his mind on a particular point is of utmost importance to training. If he allows his mind to wander it will not be sending the right sort of messages to the horse, who will then be confused. Many a fault blamed on the horse is due to his rider's lack of focus. Learning to concentrate is not easy, although some people find it less hard than others; much depends on how absorbing each rider finds his subject. One thing is certain, unless the rider trains his mind to follow a line of thought through to its conclusion, the outcome is not likely to be satisfactory.

Emotion

There is no doubt that the training process is greatly affected by the rider's emotional state. Horses can sense very quickly how their riders feel but they may not know how to respond, and this can cause them to feel anxious. How often do we take out on the horse the frustration

THE PRINCIPLES OF TRAINING

This rider and horse are obviously absorbed with each other. Note the horse 'listening' to the rider's aids.

that we feel at our own ineptitude? This is wrong, and a great part of riding skill comes from learning how to control our temper or irritation. Impatience will never produce a good result and often worsens a situation.

Nervousness too, will make us think or act negatively, which of course is of no help to anyone because riding demands positive action and firm resolve. On the other hand, over-confidence is also a mistake as this could lead the rider into a situation which has not been properly planned.

Controlling the way we think and act takes effort and is not achieved quickly, but it is all part of the jigsaw of learning to ride.

The Process of Learning for the Horse

Through the Senses

The horse uses his senses in a similar way to us, but he is disadvantaged in respect of having to use alternative methods to make himself understood. His senses inform him about what is going on around him, but it is his interpretation of these events which makes him respond as he does. Our influence in the matter is that we can cause the horse to associate either pain or pleasure with the events in his life. What the rider then has to accept and understand are the signals that the horse gives: the way he shows his resentment at being asked to do something difficult; his anxiety when he is confused or worried; his joy when he is doing what he likes. We must learn to read his mind, for only then can we satisfactorily teach him what we want him to do.

Through the Aids

The only means the rider has to communicate directly with his horse are his legs, hands, seat and voice. These four components should combine together to make the rider's intentions clear, although to start with each may have to be understood separately.

From the horse's point of view, it is his owner's voice which will first come to his notice. He will quickly learn to identify the different vocal tones, and will even recognize frequently used words, learning by association what they mean.

The influence of the rider's legs is undoubtedly very puzzling to the horse at first, but he must be taught the meaning of the various leg aids. Similarly the influence of the rider's hands may be confusing to him, particularly if they are too restrictive.

A young horse, and even some older ones, find the rider's weight disturbing: if the rider does not sit properly, the horse will lose his balance.

Rider position and use of the aids is explained in Chapter 4, but I cannot emphasize enough the importance of clear and consistent aids if the horse is to do his work well.

Through Repetition

Only by going over an exercise many times will it become firmly embedded in the horse's mind, although some will certainly learn more quickly than others. Moreover repetition is important from a physical point of view as well as a mental one, because only in this way will the horse's physique and muscle structure be progressively developed.

Repeating an exercise does not mean boring the horse to death, however! Each rider must know clearly before he begins an exercise what he wants to feel as the end result. This may only be discovered by trial and error, but when it is, he must reward the horse. Sometimes only a small improvement may take place, but this must still be rewarded even if you need to continue the exercise in order to progress further. Generally though, only a small improvement should be expected at a time.

Sometimes it is necessary to repeat an exercise until the horse is sure what is wanted; but every rider must learn when it is all right to press on and – almost more important – when it is better to stop. The horse will let his rider know this by his attitude: it will be clear when he has grasped the point, and equally clear when he is fed up with repeating an exercise.

Through Reward

There are at least six ways in which the rider can give his horse praise, and I cannot stress enough how important this aspect is in the horse's training: if he is rewarded for good work, he will remember.

THE PRINCIPLES OF TRAINING

The Voice
As already mentioned, the voice plays a big part in the horse's education: from birth onwards, the horse learns to listen and respond to it, and it should always be used to praise him even if it is accompanied by other means as well. A soothing tone can be encouraging or reassuring, which makes the horse calm and able to work better.

A Pat on the Neck
This is an excellent means of rewarding the horse and should never be underestimated. Even just a small pat is understood and appreciated – in fact, experienced riders may do no more than touch the horse quite gently on his neck in front of the withers to indicate satisfaction, but it is a gesture that the horse readily understands. Moreover it is one that can be used many times during a training session, without having to take the hand off the reins. The inside hand should be used for this purpose as it does allow a brief relaxation of contact (see Chapter 4) control being maintained by the outside hand.

A Lightening of the Aids
During training there is inevitably a greater percentage of firm aids than light

In order to learn, the horse needs constant praise. He responds well to a pat on the neck.

THE PRINCIPLES OF TRAINING

In this picture the horse is being allowed to relax and stretch, although the rider maintains a good 'contact'.

ones; but in all schooling work the aim should be lightness. This is an easing of contact following firmness, and it is in this easing that the horse gains his reward.

By Giving and Re-taking the Reins
This movement by the rider's hands allows a distinct break in the contact for a short distance. It has a calming effect, and allows the horse to 'carry himself', an important factor in achieving self-balance. It is therefore a useful training exercise, but it also constitutes a moment of freedom which is a reward in itself.

Allowing the Horse to Stretch
'Giving' the reins at any pace encourages the horse to reach outwards and downwards with his neck, and to round his back, and it can be used as a reward following a spell of hard work. It allows the horse to relax before he is asked to work again, or at the end of a lesson when he has done well. It will be most used at walk, but is perfectly feasible in trot and canter also, providing the horse is in balance. Care should always be taken to remain in control.

By Dismounting
There are always occasions in training when the horse has worked particularly well or has suddenly grasped a difficult point, and if the rider wishes to finish the

session at a good moment, it is tantamount to a reward if he dismounts; it is then quite clear to the horse that the lesson is ended and that he has done well. Obviously this policy would only be adopted when the horse is learning, and not used as a general rule.

Through Memory

The horse is renowned for his ability to recall events from any time during his life. This is an invaluable attribute as regards training, because it means that anything learned is always remembered. The disadvantage is that the horse remembers all the mistakes the rider makes, too!

One of the most useful ways to reinforce a point is to ask the horse to perform a particular exercise in the same place until it is firmly in his mind. Be careful, however, that this does not become a 'trick' which the horse will do only in that place; it should therefore be gradually incorporated elsewhere in the school so that it becomes part of the general work.

The Physical and Mental Development of the Rider

Acquiring Knowledge

Knowledge is acquired gradually over many years and the rider should be prepared for this fact; he will not suddenly find himself able to do without the help and advice of others, whether this is paid for or not. And as regards instruction, it is absolutely vital to do one's homework diligently: sporadic instruction cannot be effective unless the advice given is followed up by some hard work. Furthermore, a teacher is not there to force his pupil to work; the pupil must take what he wants from the teacher, who will respond by opening the doors of his own experience.

Fitness and Strength

However knowledgeable a rider is, he cannot use this knowledge without physical fitness. Thus he is learning to sit correctly and to apply the aids so that his horse can understand, but only by developing the correct muscles and by consistently working them can he become strong enough to ride effectively for any length of time.

Riding properly is exceedingly hard work. The experts make it look easy, but they only do so because they have spent many years training their body to perform in certain ways. It is an accepted criterion that the horse's physical development should be gradual and progressive, but so should the rider's. Strength evolves from a combination of time and effort spent working on the correct position. Often the best way to do this is by riding without stirrups, on or off the lunge; however, this should be undertaken with a certain amount of care and caution as it is easy to strain a muscle which, if damaged, may subsequently cause a great deal of trouble.

The safety angle is also most important and should always be taken into account. Thus any rider wishing to be lunged should only accept a knowledgeable person to lunge him; otherwise he may be putting himself at serious risk.

Feel

The rider will not progress if he cannot develop the right 'feel'. Feel is being

THE PRINCIPLES OF TRAINING

aware of what the horse is doing or thinking; it is largely a natural gift, and those who have it are greatly advantaged because it means they possess an instinctive perception of what is happening, or going to happen. Lack of feel is apparent by the absence of harmony between horse and rider. It can be learned, but it does take extra effort and may cause frustration.

Riding a schoolmaster is one way to acquire better feel, but for many, the only way to find it is by having it set up initially by a trainer. Riders who work on their own often worry a good deal about the feel aspect of their riding, but there is no simple answer to this, except that most do seem to recognize the right feel when it occurs because the horse suddenly manages to do what they want. This may happen by accident, however, and unless they can remember exactly what they did at the time, it can be hard to recreate. This is one reason why it is so vital to keep the brain active, and not allow yourself to drift into a non-thinking, dreamy state of mind. Concentration is essential, and only if the rider keeps his mind alert, and thinks about what is going on all the time, can feel evolve.

Self-discipline

Successful riding and training depends on self-discipline. Haphazard riding will never produce a successful result, nor will hurrying the training. Self-discipline involves a dedication to ride each day, and to work on the appropriate exercises for the stage of training. It also involves conditioning the mind to accept that work should be done by stages. Training is logical but this point is not always understood; to become a good rider, much thought should go into planning exactly the next logical step to take. Books on training will help those uncertain how to proceed, but after that it is a matter of riding every day and using the school movements to bring about the gradual development required.

Cause and Effect

Riders who can assess the reasons for a problem will be more effective than those who do not bother to work this out.

There is always a reason why a horse responds as he does; he may be too young and physically weak, or old age may have made him stiff; he may not have been taught to do what he is being asked, or he may simply be confused. His fitness will affect his ability to respond, or perhaps he is being asked to do something he cannot, because his conformation is faulty. It is the rider's responsibility to discover what the reason is so that he avoids putting himself or the horse in a difficult situation again.

The Physical and Mental Development of the Horse

Comprehension

So many problems occur simply because the horse is confused, but also because he has not been sufficiently warned beforehand. Just as the rider needs to co-ordinate his mind with his body, so does the horse, and more significantly, he does not have the advantage of the original thought. When he receives a message, his brain first has to interpret it before he can instruct his body to respond, and this process necessarily takes time; so it

THE PRINCIPLES OF TRAINING

The horse is showing apprehension, probably because the rider has asked him a question he does not understand, or is unable to answer at that moment.

The expression on the horse's face shows that he has relaxed although he has come behind the vertical.

should be clear that, when the horse is told to do something, if his rider expects an immediate reaction, he is asking the impossible!

Without due warning, therefore, the horse will not be able to do what his rider wants, when he wants; but of equal importance is the clarity with which instructions should be given. The aids are vital, and must be applied in such a way that the horse is in no doubt as to exactly what he is being asked.

Attention

As with the rider, it is very important to get the horse's mind to focus on the job in hand: if his mind is elsewhere he will not learn. The rider must provide the horse with good reason to stay alert, and that of wanting to please is usually effective: basically, if the horse thinks he will be praised for his work, he will attend to his rider far more willingly than if he receives nothing in return for his effort.

Also, and very important, is the manner in which the rider gives his messages: if they are offered in a boring or negative fashion there will be no compulsive reason for the horse to attend to them.

Lack of attention is often found in young horses, and in stallions which may be distracted by a mare in season; but whatever the age or sex of the animal, he is almost bound to lose interest if the work he is asked to do is of a dull nature. It is up to the rider to provide interesting instructions, and to keep talking to his horse via the aids.

Muscular Development

A strong physique can only be achieved through gradual and progressive development. However, the horse is not a fitness fanatic, and he doesn't have the chance to 'work out' unless his rider plans the routine and then executes it; without regular exercise and daily practice his body cannot build up, and he will be handicapped by weakness. As nearly all the work he is required to do involves a great deal of muscular effort, it is vital that he is fully prepared.

Health

A good rider will look at his horse every day and mentally assess his condition. Any feeding programme should be reviewed depending on this assessment and the necessary adjustments made. A horse cannot work properly if he carries too much weight, nor if he is 'poor'. The effort needed to carry the burden of a rider as well as to perform is far too great unless he is fit and well.

Sequence of a Lesson

1) Loosening up

The first five to ten minutes of each lesson should be devoted to allowing the horse to move forwards freely. There are different schools of thought on this matter and each rider may form his own opinion. Thus the horse may be allowed to begin with complete freedom of his head and neck with minimum contact being maintained; or he may be put 'on the bit' on a long rein and asked to go with his head low. In the latter case, his back will have the opportunity to arch and swing. Whichever method is adopted, he should not be allowed to go on the forehand. It is a good idea to rise to the trot during this period.

THE PRINCIPLES OF TRAINING

Loosening up a horse in trot.

Gathering up the horse in trot.

THE PRINCIPLES OF TRAINING

2) Bringing the horse together
Before any serious work can take place the horse must be put 'on the aids'. This means insisting that he goes forwards from the leg; and at the same time accepts the bit (see Chapter 4). Only when he is submissive to both will the rider have a chance of teaching him anything.

3) Routine work
Each day the horse should be put through his lessons of the day before to establish the work in his mind. This will also make him use his muscles in a way that will gradually make them stronger. With a very novice horse most of the exercises he knows will be used on a daily basis, but as he progresses it may be too confusing, or take too long, to go through everything that has been learned.

So long as the basics (see Chapters 6 and 7) are constantly practised, new exercises should be added gradually.

Older horses can be asked to go through most of their exercises in one session because the movements will be closely integrated, and will have been systematically developed; but even they may need to work on a specific point.

The rider should not feel daunted therefore by the belief that everything must be practised every day. He can choose what he wants to teach the horse, so long as he does not forget the fundamentals.

4) Variation
It is important for the horse mentally that he be kept alert and interested. This will only happen if his *rider* is interested in what he is doing, and makes sure that the work is not boring. Although repetition is necessary it need not be dull as long as the rider's 'conversation' to the horse via the aids is lively, not wooden (see Chapter 4).

Any variation of pace or change of exercise will aid alertness, but there must always be clear explanation and preparation in order to prevent confusion.

5) Length of lesson
A young horse may only be able to sustain the sort of effort required in schooling for twenty minutes to half an hour; an older horse should be able to go on for three-quarters of an hour to an hour. Some horses need riding for even longer, especially if extra fitness is required. The average rider and horse will probably find that half-an-hour or so is about right. However, there can be no hard and fast rules, as each individual is different as regards strength and concentration; the crucial thing to bear in mind is that it is no good going beyond the horse's individual capacity.

The rider may be guided to an extent by what he is hoping to achieve, and the ability of the horse to grasp what is wanted of him. If it has taken ten minutes to teach him something, then leave it at that; he will remember it all the better the next time.

6) Finishing a lesson
As far as the horse is concerned, the most important thing is that he ends his lesson in a happy frame of mind so that he looks forward to his work the following day. The way to make sure of this is always to end 'on the crest of the wave', when something has gone really well.

7) Cooling off
This is an important part of equitation although it is not specifically related to the work. Muscles need to relax and cool

THE PRINCIPLES OF TRAINING

down from the exertion of work, so a period of relaxed movement at walk on a long rein is a good way to do this before returning to the stable. The horse may be ridden, or led round with his stirrups run up and a loosened girth, depending on his owner's preference.

Progress

Many riders are puzzled by how much progress to expect of their horse and in what space of time. The answer, I am afraid, is bound to be ambiguous as every horse and rider varies to such an extent. All I can say is that anyone wanting to be successful at any sport should anticipate years rather than months. If this can be accepted at the outset, disappointment and frustration may be minimized. Neither horse nor rider can shoot to fame in a week or two, and even the simplest competition requires a lot of work.

Training Problems Affecting the Rider

Teaching oneself is not easy, and I felt it might be helpful to mention a few of the problems that all riders face.

Dedication

However gifted or enthusiastic a rider is, he will need to be dedicated to what he is doing, and this means working hard. Training a horse properly is not a half-hour job twice a week, it is a daily commitment. Furthermore any horse has his own whims, and like us, sometimes he feels good and sometimes he doesn't. Being able to cope with his moods as well as our own changing emotions is a huge test, and one which will need continuing resolve.

Determination

Determination goes hand in hand with dedication, but it is easy to feel inadequate or despondent if things fail to go right, say, at some competition. However, at these times it is as well to remember what inspired the original ambition and to put all failure into perspective. I know from my own experience that seemingly insuperable mountains can be climbed and conquered, and that if a person is determined to succeed he will do so.

Inconsistency

Being inconsistent, either as a result of erratic thought or because of a haphazardly organized training routine, will never bring good results. The horse will always be confused, and physically he will not be able to develop in the right way.

A Negative Attitude

It is not always easy to be positive, but it is important to have a definite outlook and to apply the aids with resolve so that the horse realizes he must do what he is asked. Nervousness makes riders negative, and this is not easy to overcome. It must be remembered that the horse is generally aware of how we feel, and if a rider is weak the horse may take advantage of him or her, or will simply do what *he* wants because a clear instruction is not given to him.

THE PRINCIPLES OF TRAINING

Training Problems Affecting the Horse

Muddled Response

Throughout his training the horse will make mistakes. If he seems confused, or fails to offer the correct response to an aid, the rider must ask himself whether he gave the right signals, and if he gave them clearly.

Hurried Training

Unless the horse is taken through his training patiently, with intelligent use of the exercises available for systematic progress, he may well struggle. He will manifest his problems by resisting, and then his rider must learn to 'read the signs', and if necessary start again.

When the Pressure is On!

If a rider is ambitious or even over-anxious about some problem he may put considerable pressure on the horse, believing this to be the way through the difficulty. Some horses can take pressure perfectly well and may accept it, others will become even more anxious and confused. It is the rider's responsibility to know how much pressure his horse can take, and how readily he will crack up under the nervous strain.

There are moments in training when it is necessary to press on with a particular exercise, or to push the horse on in his work, but in general, less experienced riders should proceed with care and avoid unnecessary confrontation.

CHAPTER 4
Rider Position and the Aids

The results you want can only be obtained if you have an effective influence over the horse. For this reason there is an accepted position in the saddle from which the aids can be applied in the best way.

Some areas of the horse's anatomy are more sensitive than others; one is around the mouth, and another is around the girth area. If the rider's legs and hands (via the bit) are used in certain ways, these sensitive areas are alerted and a response can be expected. The way to use the aids will be explained later in this chapter; the matter of first importance is to establish the correct position in the saddle.

This rider is sitting quite well for flat work although she could be more central in the saddle.

RIDER POSITION AND THE AIDS

Rider sitting well in jumping length and showing good contact through the legs and hands.

Rider Position

First, it is essential to have a saddle that allows the rider to sit in the centre, and doesn't tip the body forwards or backwards. This can be seen quite easily if the saddle is placed on the horse's back; any undue slope either way may cause problems. Also, it is most important to have a saddle that not only fits the horse properly but is the right size for the rider's seat. It is just as bad to be floating about in one that is too large as it is to be 'pegged' into a small one!

It is usually apparent when a rider first sits on a horse as to whether he has natural talent. Those who have, automatically sit in a relaxed manner and have no difficulty in adopting the right position. Stiffness or tension will make sitting awkward and will certainly make giving the aids very difficult.

Once positioned in the centre of the saddle, the rider should relax his seat muscles and seek to find his seat bones, which should be open and not clenched together. He should then give attention to his hips which should be angled, with the topmost part of the hip bone tipped forwards, not backwards. This initial position of the seat allows the spine to be slightly curved but upright, and allows for flexibility of the waist which needs to absorb the movement of the horse.

RIDER POSITION AND THE AIDS

Hips tipped forward.

Hips tipped backwards.

In addition, if the rider sits in this way his thigh can be held in a flat position against the saddle, with the fat part of the leg being underneath the thigh and therefore not hindering a close contact. If the thigh is flat to the saddle, the lower leg (from the knee downwards) can curve round the horse's belly, giving the rider maximum contact with the sensitive area by the girth.

All joints should be flexible, so it is a mistake to force the heel down too strictly; but it should be borne in mind that in order to brace the calf muscles, the heel does need to be lower than the toe.

The arms should be held in a relaxed position close to the body, but should have great flexibility and must be independent of the seat. Whilst the body and leg position should be maintained, the arms should be able to follow the movement of the horse's head and neck; they are a pliable connection between the rider's body and the mouth of the horse.

The head of the rider should be upright because if it drops, its weight can drag the shoulders forwards, thus weakening the spine. It should not be held up stiffly, but nor should it adopt any unsightly nodding, like a chicken pecking grain!

The hands should be held above the horse's withers and slightly to each side, with the thumbs upmost and pointing towards each other. The wrists should be supple, and should never be held in a stiff, rounded position. The fingers should be closed, but should have an elastic hold on the reins.

The Natural Aids

Use of the Seat

It is crucial that the rider's seat exerts the correct influence, and to this end it is most important that the seat bones and hips maintain their position. Tension from the seat muscles prevents the rider from being able to sit deep, which he needs to do

RIDER POSITION AND THE AIDS

Because the legs are 'drawn up', the influence of the seat and lower leg is weakened.

in order to have the maximum contact and effect. The seat should be sufficiently relaxed that it follows the horse's movement, and sufficiently strong that it stays close to the horse at all times. 'Shovelling' of the seat is unattractive and is not effective, and although the words 'push' and 'drive' are used in association with sending the horse forwards, this action of strength only occurs from a bracing of the back which sends the seat into the saddle.

The seat bones should take equal pressure when the horse is straight, but there may be more on one than on the other at certain times. Specific aids, and using the body weight, will be explained later in this chapter, but in general terms the rider should consider his weight in relation to balance as a whole, and sit accordingly.

Use of the Legs

The rider's legs will be the main incentive for the horse to go forwards. They should be kept close to the horse's sides, with the lower leg (from the knee downwards) just behind the girth. The best guide for assessing the position is that the stirrup leather should be perpendicular to the ground.

The horse should be taught to respond to a light pressure, but this may take him some time to learn. Initially he does so from the feel of a schooling whip used at the same moment as the leg aid.

A rider should refrain from kicking his horse along; not only is this tedious and irritating to the horse, it is also ineffective. Instead he must learn to brace his

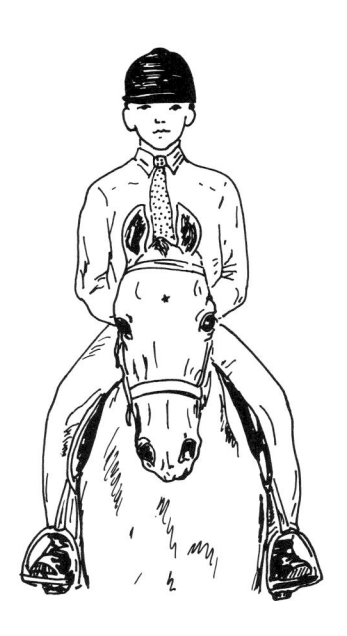

RIDER POSITION AND THE AIDS

Good leg contact, with toes pointing forwards.

The knee and toe of the rider are turned outwards causing the leg to come too far back and away from the horse.

Poor leg contact, with knees and toes pointing out.

calf muscles so that when the leg is used it can be felt by the horse. Combined with the whip, the message from the rider's legs alerts the horse into a response.

Once the horse understands the leg aids, the whip should only be used only minimally, to reinforce the natural aid.

Use of the Upper Body

Flopping about or leaning forwards or backwards will cause both horse and rider to be unbalanced. The spine should be upright so that the vertebrae sit securely one on top of each other, wherein lies their strength.

The rider's shoulders should be in line with the horse's shoulders, so that when turns or circles are ridden they remain

RIDER POSITION AND THE AIDS

By leaning forwards and pressing on the stirrups the rider has caused her seat to come out of the saddle and her ankles to be rigid.

parallel. A common fault is for the outside shoulder of the rider to be 'left behind', which will make it difficult to maintain the accuracy of a bend.

Another fault which occurs frequently is that the rider collapses at his waist – normally to the inside – so that his upper body is leaning over. This is a hindrance both to balance and to the effect of the seat.

Round shoulders are a deportment fault; moreover when riding, this attitude allows the head to fall forwards which looks ugly, and it also weakens the influence of the back.

The rider's head should be held up and he should look forwards between his horse's ears. When turning or circling he should turn the head to see where he wants to go, but at no time should it be held to the side.

Use of the Hands

The rider's hands bear a tremendous responsibility because they control the horse. Although basically their optimum position is just above the horse's withers, they must necessarily be extremely flexible. This does not mean that they should wave around, indeed they should be kept as still as possible – though never rigid – so that the horse does not get jerked in his mouth.

RIDER POSITION AND THE AIDS

Too strong or sudden pressure on the horse's mouth may cause him to throw up his head or open his mouth.

There are many occasions in training when one or both of the hands need raising, or they may need to be held further forwards in front of the withers. One thing they should never do is to pull backwards, or have a resisting tension on the reins. It is also important that the shoulders, arms and wrists of the rider are relaxed, otherwise tension will travel through them to the hands, which will then be unable to hold the reins in a sensitive fashion. So often a horse's work is spoilt because the rider hangs onto the reins to balance himself, or because he lacks sympathy with his mouth. If every rider put himself in his horse's place, imagining what it would be like to have a bit in his mouth, many horses would be ridden better.

Many riders find the subject of the correct length of rein a baffling question. The answer is not simple, but as a guide, if the hands are placed in a designated position, for instance just above and in front of the withers, the length of rein will be determined by the contact the rider can keep with his horse's mouth without altering his hands.

RIDER POSITION AND THE AIDS

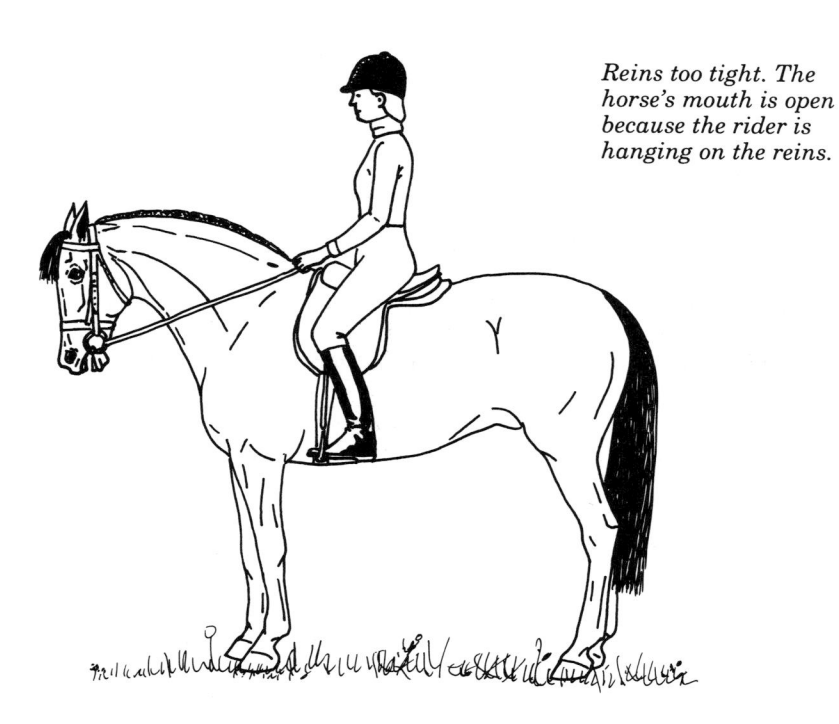

Reins too tight. The horse's mouth is open because the rider is hanging on the reins.

Reins too loose. The horse is half asleep.

RIDER POSITION AND THE AIDS

The Aids

The natural aids – the legs, hands, body-weight and voice of the rider – can be backed up by artificial aids from time to time if needed. There is also the horse's natural communication system. The rider must necessarily teach his horse what response he expects of him, and to do this he must be consistent; for example it would be very muddling to us if we were taught on Monday that two plus two equal four, and on Thursday that it equals five! This would be illogical and wrong. Thus the rider must be clear in his mind what aid he is giving for a particular exercise, and then be diligent in giving the same one each time.

Communicating with the Horse

Contact

The whole communication system between a rider and his horse depends on the rider's ability to take a contact, maintain it, and use it effectively. By contact, I mean two things. First, the rider must be able to sit in such a way that his legs can wrap themselves round the horse, thus giving maximum contact with his body. Second, he must be able to hold the reins so that he maintains a constant elastic tension between his hands and the horse's mouth. This contact puts the horse in a position where he can best listen to the aids he is given. He is then between the leg and hand of the rider.

Maintaining contact correctly takes years to achieve as it is a sensitive matter and one that the rider has to learn to feel. His legs must be firm, but should not be used in order to grip himself onto the saddle, and his hands must not be used for balance. Developing a secure position in the saddle will prevent this from happening.

Coordination

People vary enormously in their ability to coordinate mind and limb. Natural flair is a big advantage and will make the task easier, and those who are fortunate enough to possess it will automatically use their seat, legs and hands in such a way that these are not in opposition to each other. By this I mean that if the seat and legs ask the horse to go forwards, the hands must allow him to obey and should not prevent him, as so often happens. In fact it seems to be quite a common occurrence that the rider's seat, legs and hands give opposing messages, and although unintentional, this is very confusing for the horse. Every rider should give this matter a great deal of thought, especially if his horse is not doing what he wants.

In more advanced equitation, coordination in the aids becomes even more vital as the horse is being asked to do one thing closely followed by another. In dressage competitions or when jumping a course of fences, this matters a great deal. A lack of co-ordination can be felt in several ways:

- Difficulty in achieving a movement.
- Resistance by the horse.
- The rider's lack of balance in the saddle and dependency on the reins for support.
- The horse's lack of balance due to intermittent rein contact or loss of rein contact altogether, or the rider's unsteady position.

RIDER POSITION AND THE AIDS

- Inability on the part of the rider to make himself clear.

To improve poor coordination, the rider should first have a clear idea of his aim; next, he should plan it carefully; then execute it patiently.

Conversation

The way the rider 'talks' to his horse through the aids is of utmost importance: this is only possible by first achieving good contact. Coordinated messages will then travel from the rider's brain to his limbs and be transmitted to the horse's brain. These messages can be of varying types:

The interesting message
This alerts the horse and makes him listen to his rider. It is achieved by the rider first using his legs to promote attention and energy, and is then followed by a feel-and-ease action of the hands. Although the hands are held in a closed position they should never be clasped shut but should be held relaxed, so that a slight opening or closing of the fingers can tighten or ease the rein tension.

Varying the tension on the rein will keep the horse's mouth alive and his mind active. It should be subtle, and as such is only a matter for each horse and his rider; it should not be obvious to anyone watching.

The dull message
This lacks purpose and has no 'feel-and-ease' process; in other words, there is effectively no contact at all.

Many people ride aimlessly, with no real idea of what they want to achieve. However, before even getting on to the horse there should be a plan for the day, and for those riders who are unsure how to proceed, a little study beforehand would not go amiss. Lack of purpose and this sort of 'dead' contact will lead to the horse becoming thoroughly bored, and very soon a frustrated rider.

The intermittent message
This begins all right, has a lapse, and then recovers. During the lapse the rider loses concentration, and the horse is left to his own devices. His instinctive sense of self-preservation will come to his rescue, and he will behave on his own initiative; but this course of action will then be interrupted by the rider resuming his original instruction. The result is confusion, and it may also lead quite quickly to irritation, as the horse is then prevented from following his natural inclination.

The harsh message or rough aid
This is given without due thought, or with insufficient preparation, and its effect is very often a sudden jab in the horse's mouth. Obviously this is unpleasant for him and he will show his resentment by opening his mouth or flinging up his head to avoid the pain of the bit.

The unyielding message
This is when a rider simply hangs on to the horse's mouth and makes no attempt to 'feel-and-ease' at all. In this circumstance the horse will usually pull back or lean on his rider's hands; there is very little else he can do!

This is similar to the dull message, but it contains an unpleasant restrictive ingredient which the horse is bound to find objectionable.

The negative message
Here, the horse is left wondering what to

RIDER POSITION AND THE AIDS

do! In this situation he will probably make up his own mind, which may not be what his rider intended. The outcome is often irritation and impatience on the part of the rider, causing subsequent distress to the horse.

Riders who are nervous are often responsible for giving negative messages or ones that are simply vague, as they are themselves unsure. Clearly this is of no benefit at all to the horse, and a more positive approach is needed.

Aids for Specific Movements

Each hand and leg of the rider has its own particular job to do, and in this respect they have the same capacity in every movement ridden, with just small variations in degree of pressure which indicate to the horse the movement required. Thus to go in a straight line, the rider's legs should maintain an even contact against the horse's body, and his hands should do the same with the horse's mouth. The legs should then make the horse go forwards and the reins will steer him, as if riding up a narrow corridor.

When turning or circling, the aids become more detailed, as follows: the outside rein is responsible for determining the route and maintaining direction, and controlling the horse's speed.

The inside rein asks for and maintains a flexion to the direction in which the horse is going; thus if he is being asked to circle right he should look to the right.

The inside leg generates more bend in the horse's body when it is needed, and it keeps the horse going forwards into the controlling outside rein.

The outside leg prevents the hindquarters from falling or swinging outwards; it keeps the quarters curved round the inside leg when bend is required; and it helps the inside leg to maintain impulsion.

The rider's weight should be evenly balanced on the horse, but it may be used to assist or correct the horse's balance during his work by bringing more pressure onto a particular seat-bone. This must be assessed at the time. For example, there are moments such as in a canter strike-off when bringing weight onto the inside seat-bone assists that leg to come more round the horse; or during a half-pass, to help take the horse in the direction you want to go. For the more novice rider the weight should not be considered overmuch, because using it incorrectly can so easily upset the horse's balance.

Going Forwards

It is not easy to decide how much leg pressure to use, but be guided by the response the horse makes. If there is none, clearly he has not been conscious of any pressure at all! The lower leg should close when giving an aid, and if the horse ignores it, a schooling whip should make him realize that he is being asked a question. Avoid the continuous squeeze, as this will have no effect. Also, never flap the legs against the horse's sides. He should respond to one squeeze followed by an easing of pressure, or a quick vibration of the heel (not drawn upwards) may have more effect.

Riders should also be ready to give the horse a good positive kick in moments of crisis or when particular reinforcement is needed, and the horse must be taught to respond; but to kick him too often merely serves to deaden his response.

RIDER POSITION AND THE AIDS

Turning

Many riders seem to be unaware that a horse cannot turn at right angles, nor can he perform an acute angle. He can pirouette on his hindquarters, but that is something different (see Chapter 8). When turning, the horse must first go forwards, otherwise it is rather like expecting a car to turn with the hand brake still on! It is common practice with novice riders to try to turn their horse from halt. The result is a haul on the reins, with the horse struggling round with his head in the air! Similarly, many such riders try to trot or canter at an angle of 45 degrees and wonder why the horse falls over or stops!

A horse needs to be prepared for a turn by the rider taking a slight flexion to the direction in which he will be required to go; the outside rein and inside leg then prevent the turn from taking place until the designated point has been reached.

Transitions

In all transition – changes from one pace to another – the horse should be ridden forwards from the seat and legs. In upward transitions, the hands will allow the horse to move forwards by an easing of the contact, and in all downward ones, the hands will restrain the forward energy.

Transitions should be smooth and ridden gradually. A horse cannot stop suddenly, he needs preparation: an abrupt reduction of energy results in loss of balance and resistance against what is probably a harsh aid.

Upward transitions are generally easier than downward ones, as the hindquarters lift the horse when he is going forwards, but tend not to stay engaged when coming down in the paces, so the horse falls on his forehand. This is a worry to many riders, who find it difficult to keep their position at this moment. Time and practice, and being aware of the need to use the legs to keep the horse engaged will bring about improvement.

Obedience

Throughout training, the rider's co-ordination and the horse's submission to the aids are of paramount importance (see Chapter 7): only in this way can harmony between the two develop. Obtaining the required responses from the horse is not always simple because there is much to be considered; but every rider should set himself a standard at a suitable level, to which both he and the horse conform. This standard may be determined by watching others at that level, thus finding out what he might reasonably expect from himself and his horse.

Having set his parameters, the rider should then insist that his horse does what he wants, when he wants it. This does not mean that he has any sudden and irrational expectations of his horse, merely that he requires a response as the result of a well prepared instruction.

Obedience should never make the horse downhearted or dispirited; it should evolve from a united effort in which the horse is glad to please.

The Artificial Aids

The Whip

Although this is classed as an artificial

aid, its use in training is invaluable as a reinforcement to the rider's leg aids. Many riders shy away from its use, however, or maintain that they cannot use it because their horse is frightened of it. I know this can be quite a problem, but I also know it can be overcome.

If your horse is frightened of the whip it is important to be patient and to spend time making him less fearful. In the stable, let him look at it and smell it, making sure it is kept still. Reassure him with the voice and a pat on the neck. When he is less nervous, ride with a short whip, although don't use it, and don't change it from one hand to the other. On a different day, ride with it in the other hand. Much later, use the same procedure with a long whip. Next, practise resting the end of the whip on the horse's flank, all the while reassuring him. Eventually, and with a great deal of patience, the horse will accept its use.

Spurs

Some competitions actually demand that spurs be worn, and in some show classes it is accepted dress. However, the spur should be considered as something to help in the 'fine tuning' of leg aids; it should not be used as a substitute for correct training.

Some lazy horses may need a spur to help the rider's legs wake them up and keep them going. Also, riders with very big strong horses may need to use spurs to help them engage the hindquarters.

There is no harm in riders using spurs so long as they remember that they are to help them train the horse better, and not simply to make him go!

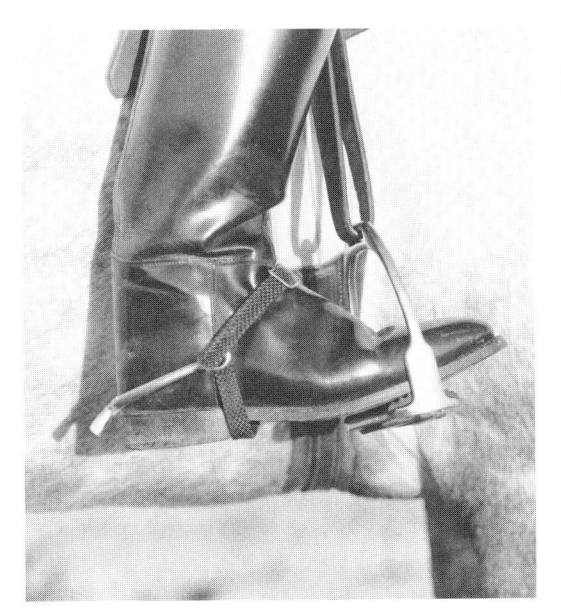

If spurs are worn in this manner they cannot be of any assistance to the legs.

Although the position of this spur is more likely to help the leg aids it is still worn too low. The arm of the spur should be where the horizontal seam of the boot is.

RIDER POSITION AND THE AIDS

A running martingale that is properly fitted will not interfere with the horse.

Martingales

I shall only discuss the running martingale in this book because, in my experience, a standing martingale has no purpose from a training point of view. A running martingale, on the other hand, does have some value used on a horse which has learned to go with his head excessively high; the rider then has at least some assistance while he is trying to make improvements.

It should be remembered that the martingale will have to be removed at some point and that the horse must ultimately be able to go without it.

Running reins

On the whole, running or draw reins should be avoided for the simple reason that they cover a fault but do not necessarily help to correct it; nevertheless they can play a useful part in the horse's training. They are particularly worthwhile used as a corrective measure on a horse which persistently carries his head high in the air and becomes too strong to control. They should be used for only a limited period, however, as eventually the horse must do his work without them.

CHAPTER 5

Lungeing and Long-Reining

In this chapter I shall try to show why lungeing and long-reining are so useful in training. There are four main occasions when lunge and long reins are used:

1. Training the young horse.
2. Exercising or re-training the older horse.
3. Teaching the rider.
4. Teaching the horse to jump.

Initial Handling and Preparation

Particularly with a youngster, the owner should, before starting any work at all, have ensured that his horse is well prepared. His initial handling is all-important, and he should have been well handled from foalhood when a bond of respect, not fear, should have been formed. A foal should be prepared to obey his owner, and allow himself to be led, brushed and have his feet picked up. These early lessons are so important to him and to the general rapport.

When the youngster is about three years old, depending on growth, he should learn to wear a roller in the stable. This should not be tightened suddenly, which might cause alarm, but it must be tight enough so that it does not slip. This is crucial, as many problems in saddling can be traced back to this first experience.

When the horse is confident in his roller, a cavesson may be introduced. Its heavy weight and the noise of the rings may take a little getting used to, but most horses don't mind them.

Before the youngster is actually lunged, which will be the first step towards ridden training, he may also have to become used to a breastplate to keep the roller in place, and boots which he will need to wear to protect his legs. To eliminate any worry, all new items of equipment should be introduced to the horse gradually, allowing him to see, smell and touch them; in this way he will make his own assessment and will have time to learn about and accept each new experience.

Just as the horse needs to be prepared, so should the owner. He should have had at least one lesson to learn lungeing technique, and also how to avoid pitfalls. He must know how to hold the lunge line, what to do with the whip, where to stand and how to move. This is all most important to training, and especially from the point of view of safety. He must appreciate the hazards of lungeing wearing spurs, and understand the necessity for gloves.

Lungeing Situations

Lungeing the Young Horse

The horse, dressed correctly, should be

LUNGEING AND LONG-REINING

brought into an enclosed safe area, preferably with a soft but not slippery surface. On his first lesson he will probably be wearing just boots and a cavesson with the lunge attached to the front ring on top of the nose. His trainer should be wearing gloves and sensible footwear with non-slip soles, and he should have the lunge coiled up and held in his left hand; it must never be tightly wrapped round the hand, but should be in a position such that it can either be held easily, or can be slipped off the fingers for release (*see* diagram). The whip should be held under the arm with the thong pointing away from the horse.

The horse should be led to the middle of the circle where he is to be lunged and should stand quietly, facing the direction he is to go while the trainer moves back to stand by his shoulder. Some people like an assistant to stand by the horse's head to start with, and may require him to lead the horse round. The assistant should stand behind the lunge line, and when he is not required he should move in towards the centre of the circle where he can be of use if needed.

The trainer will then form a triangle with the lunge line, the horse and the whip as the three sides, and himself as the centre point, from which position he is best able to control the horse. The horse should then be asked to walk forwards, to halt and to walk again until he understands. He may be asked for a trot if the trainer feels he is in control. This should be done on each rein.

The horse will be confused at first and may try to stop or turn in and the trainer must be skilful enough to position himself where he can drive the horse forwards at once, thus avoiding a problem. When the horse is asked to halt and stand he should not turn in but should wait for his next instruction. The trainer should walk up to the horse on the circle perimeter, coiling up the lunge as he goes and putting the whip behind him where it will not alarm the horse. The horse should never be allowed to get excited or frightened, as he may easily get out of control and either hurt himself or the trainer.

As lungeing progresses, the horse should perform trot work and transitions, and later a canter should be included. He should not be allowed to choose his speed, but should listen to his trainer's voice, from which he will learn the words of command. These words will form a basis of understanding from which, later on, the horse will learn to associate the aids when ridden. He will quickly pick up the meaning, providing the trainer keeps consistently to a particular word, using the same tone each time.

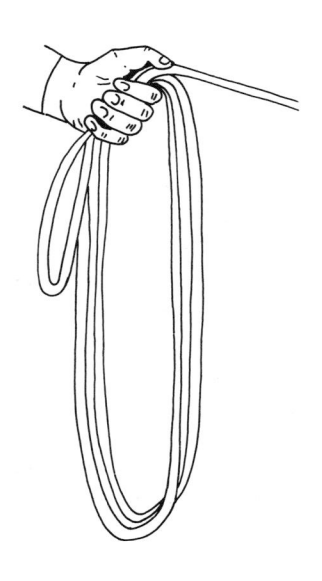

Lungeing rein held in the left hand for easy release.

LUNGEING AND LONG-REINING

The horse is moving forwards calmly, freely and in a round outline. The trainer is well positioned.

The circle size should be dictated by the amount of control the trainer has. It may of necessity have to start quite small, but should soon be enlarged to 15m or even larger. The trainer must, however, be in a position to regulate the steps of the horse and to encourage the correct curve according to the circle. He must also be able to see whether the horse's hind legs are following in the track of the forelegs and whether there is sufficient activity of the hind legs (see Chapter 6). From the ground, he is in a good position to note any irregularities, loss of rhythm of the steps or unlevelness of stride. It is important to avoid allowing too much curve of the horse's neck to the inside, but he should not adopt an outside bend, either.

Hollowing of the top line is a bad fault, but it can be prevented by using side reins; these should be attached to the rings on either side of the cavesson, and the other ends fixed to rings on the roller. After the first few lessons, it is a good idea to use side reins anyway, which should be tight enough to encourage the horse to lower his head and round his back. One word of warning. When the horse first feels himself 'trapped' by the feel of side reins he may panic and try to run back, or fall over. As soon as they are attached, the trainer must be in the right position to quickly send the horse forwards. Once accustomed to them, however, most horses do not object.

The side reins give the horse his first

taste of being 'brought together', which the rider's legs and hands will do when he is ridden. As soon as he is confident, the roller may be replaced by a saddle with the stirrups secured so that they cannot dangle and frighten the horse, and a bridle may be put on under the cavesson. The side reins may now be transferred to the bit and should be of equal length.

A mild snaffle bit should be used, held in place by a correctly fitted flash noseband. This prevents the horse from opening his mouth and discovering ways to evade the bit. So many ridden problems stem from the fact that the horse was allowed the chance to get his tongue over the bit when he was first bridled.

A horse should not be lunged for too long at a time because constant circling imposes great strain on his joints and tendons. Ten minutes on each rein is certainly enough to start with.

Lungeing for Training

As the horse gets older, he may be taught more things on the lunge. He will already have learned to walk, trot and canter on the correct lead in both directions. He should know how to balance and hold a rhythm. He should have been taught not to lean on the lunge, but to keep on a circle whilst maintaining just a light contact with his trainer; this may be achieved by giving a firm pull on the lunge rein attached to the cavesson, followed by a lightening. He should have learned to stand square, and to make smooth transitions.

Further exercises may include spiralling, where the horse is drawn in on the circle and then sent out for the purpose of improving his balance and control over himself. Lengthening may also be done in trot and in canter for a few strides at a time.

Throughout this work the trainer must make sure that the horse keeps a round outline, which encourages the correct muscle development; this may help to avoid a great deal of difficulty later on when he is ridden. He should also be learning to accept his lessons calmly and without tension, a factor so destructive to the quality of the paces (see Chapter 5).

Lungeing for Fitness

In order to build up strength, lungeing may be useful not only for a young horse but an older one also, as long as it is done in the right way – that is, steady work at a sensible speed. It should not take the place of roadwork or schooling, but should be used in addition to these, when extra fitness is required. It can be a useful variation to riding.

Lungeing for Exercise

Sometimes it is necessary to use lungeing as an alternative to riding for such reasons as the ill-health of the rider, or perhaps to allow the horse to recover from a sore back. It means that the horse can be kept partially fit and ready to ride again.

Young horses may need the freedom of a few moments on a lunge before they are ridden. Although they should not be out of control, they may be allowed to express enthusiasm or get rid of excess energy by a squeal and a buck, so long as this does not endanger anybody.

Lungeing for Re-Schooling Purposes

Older horses, or horses that have been

spoilt, may benefit from work on the lunge. It gives the trainer an opportunity to see exactly what the problems are, and the horse the chance to improve without the hindrance of a rider. Most problems with older horses have to do with stiffness, or resistance because their mouth has been spoilt, and lungeing on side reins can be a great help in improving these problems. It is less exhausting for the rider, and easier for the horse to get over his difficulties than if he were ridden.

The use of a Chambon is such cases may bring improvement as it encourages rounding and loosening of the horse's back, the site of many stiffnesses.

Sensible work can be a help to the horse mentally and therapeutic to him physically, because it increases the blood supply and strengthens weak muscles

Whenever the horse is being lunged, the trainer must keep a strict eye on the state of its feet. Lungeing without shoes is all right for a while on a soft surface, but otherwise the hooves will quickly suffer wear without them. If shod, a close eye should be kept on clenches as the horse can readily injure himself on a circle. Also, excessive wear may mean that when the horse puts his foot down it is on an unlevel bearing surface, which would be bad for joints and tendons.

It is very important to cool the horse off in the normal way at the end of a lunge lesson. If he has become hot and is put straight back into his stable, his muscles could tie up as a result.

Lungeing to Teach the Horse to Jump

Many riders may prefer to wait until their horse is ridden before they introduce it to jumping, but lungeing over poles or small fences can be a very good way to start.

The horse must first of all be competent

Loose jumping is a good way to teach the horse to look after himself.

in his basic lunge work; he should be calm and obedient. Begin by placing one pole on the long side of a school, and ask the horse first to walk over it, then to trot. The trainer can then lunge the horse using his normal circle, and when he wishes to use the pole, he moves nearer to it until the track of the circle passes over it.

If the trainer is agile enough, poles may be put down in a straight line approximately 4ft (1.2m) apart depending on the horse's length of stride; he may then be asked to negotiate these with his trainer alongside. This is a useful exercise as it makes him look where he is going, and should teach him to pick up his feet. Once he has gone over the poles, the trainer can resume a circle before positioning himself and the horse for another attempt.

Poles may also be laid on a circle 2ft 9in (0.83m) apart on the inner side and 3ft 3in (1m) at the outer; these may be built up in number, which will teach the horse to work in a nice round shape over them. At all times he should be able to lower his head, stretch his neck and round his back.

Once the horse is calm and confident over poles, cavaletti may be substituted for one or more poles, and the horse should trot over them. These should not be more than 12in (30cm) high, and great care should be taken not to allow the lunge line to get caught on the arm of the cavaletti.

During this work it is probably best if the lunge line is attached to the cavesson and not to the bit, to avoid any jerk in the horse's mouth which might put him off.

The trainer must be prepared to be firm, to give encouragement, keep up impulsion and help the horse to use his own brain power. If he presents the horse at the pole or cavaletti properly, the horse will learn to look after himself.

Lungeing the Rider

This may be done for two reasons: to teach a beginner how to sit and establish a secure position; or to improve a rider who has developed problems. Nearly all riders have a strong and weak side, and they may develop a particular fault which they find hard to eradicate, and which affects the way they sit or give the aids. For this reason, early work on the lunge is good for them.

Riding without stirrups and/or reins encourages the development of balance and builds up muscles in the right way. It is hard for the rider to correct wrongly developed muscles, as it is for the horse, and may take a long time.

It is absolutely essential that a rider only allows himself to be lunged by someone with experience, and on a suitable horse. Then he can give his undivided concentration to improving his position and the way he uses the aids. He may need to do exercises to improve balance and suppleness, such as circling with the arms, touching the toes, stretching the legs, and so on. This can be quite fun, as well as beneficial.

Learning to jump on the lunge is a good opportunity to practise following the movement of the horse without interfering with it. It teaches the rider what to do when the unexpected happens, and how to sit. Because the trainer is in control the rider does not have to worry, and therefore confidence can be built up.

Long Reining

The object of long reining is to teach the horse as much as possible before it is sat on. It provides the trainer with the opportunity to send the horse forwards into the bridle and to teach him what the bit means.

Before a bridle is used, the two lines can be attached to either side of the cavesson, coming to the hands via rings on either side of the roller. Some trainers do not use a roller but bring the reins directly to their hands. There is a danger that the horse may become tangled up unless the reins are kept taut – but long reining is not a job for a novice in any case. Another alternative is to bring the reins through the stirrups of the saddle, providing these are held securely.

Once the reins are attached to the bit, the trainer can teach the horse how to be controlled: to start, stop and turn and generally listen to the rein aids. These will be used in conjunction with the voice commands already learned on the lunge, so there should be no confusion. The contact from the hands to the horse's mouth should be the same as when he is ridden, so that he learns the messages he will be required to accept.

Pulling on the reins or jabbing at the horse's mouth will do him no good and will make the ridden job harder.

There are many exercises that the horse can be asked to do. Of course, he should be taught to go in straight lines as the long reins are ideal for this purpose, but circles and school figures (see Chapter 8) can be described, as long as the trainer is fit and active.

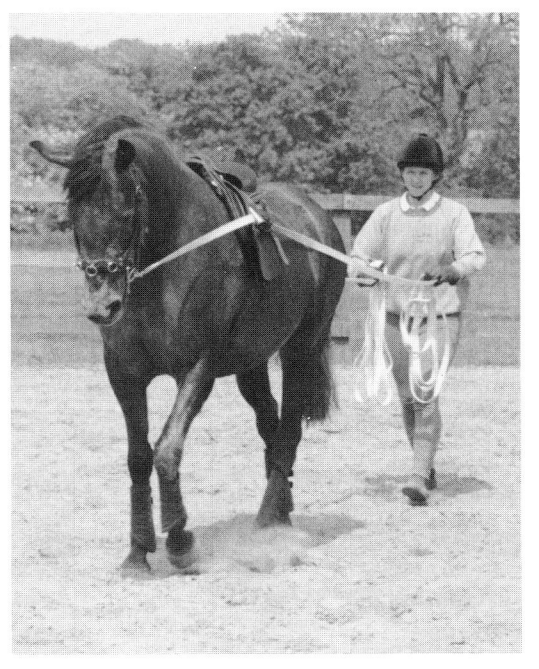

If done properly, long reining is a good way to teach the horse the meaning of the bit.

Driving the horse in this way builds up muscle in the hindquarters, it teaches him to use his hind legs under his body and can, if done properly, develop a correct rounded outline.

CHAPTER 6

The Horse's Paces

The horse's paces are the basis of his entire training, therefore their correct development is vital. Not only must the rider be able to increase the capacity of the paces, which will enhance their quality, he must also preserve the correct sequence of steps. It is all too easy, from hurried training or ignorance, to spoil the natural ability of the horse.

The Sequence of Footfalls in the Paces

The correct sequence of footfalls is the first essential to grasp when learning about the paces. Each one is different, and may be identified as follows:

The Walk

The walk is a four-beat movement in which each footfall is separate; this gives it a counting rhythm of one, two, three, four in quick succession.

The Trot

This is a two-beat movement, the horse touching the ground with one pair of diagonal legs (for example the off fore and the near hind together), followed by a moment of suspension, followed by the other pair of diagonal legs (near-fore and off-hind) touching the ground.

When rising to the trot, the rider rises when one diagonal pair of legs touches the ground and sits when the opposite pair does so. This is called riding *on* a diagonal (not to be confused with riding *a* diagonal when you cross the school diagonally in order to change the rein). To keep the horse's back muscles even, the rider should alter the diagonal each time he changes the rein; thus if he starts by rising on the off-fore, near-hind diagonal and sitting on the near-fore, off-hind diagonal on the right rein, when he changes to the left rein he should sit for one extra stride and then re-start the rise when he will find himself sitting and rising on the opposite diagonal to when he started.

The Canter

The canter is a three-beat movement. In a true canter when he is being ridden on a circle, the horse starts the canter stride with his outside hind leg, follows it with the inside hind leg and outside foreleg together, and finishes the stride with the inside foreleg. He then has a moment of suspension when he is off the ground before the sequence starts again.

When watching a horse in each of his paces it is important to train the eye to see these sequences so that any irregularities of rhythm or length of stride are noticed immediately.

THE HORSE'S PACES

The rider has hurried the horse out of the true rhythm of the walk.

A good trot in a nice round outline.

THE HORSE'S PACES

Although this canter is 'croup high', which is incorrect (the hindquarters should be lowered), it does show the period of suspension.

A lengthened canter which, although it is somewhat 'hollow', shows a clear moment of suspension.

There are many features of the paces that it is important both to be able to see and, even more significantly, to feel. Each pace presents different problems, but before I go into these I want to describe some of the ingredients common to all.

The Quality of the Paces

Going Forwards

Unless the horse is going forwards in the first place there will be nothing to work on. It sounds common sense, but this subject is often misunderstood. The first point to understand is that it has nothing to do with speed; going faster is not necessarily 'going forwards' in the way it is required in training. What it means is that the horse is sufficiently active in his joints, with the hindquarters working energetically under his body, that he can propel himself along with springing steps and a supple back. At the same time he must be submissive to the bit.

Balance

Only if there is overall balance will the horse be able to perform properly (see Chapter 7). Any alteration in his balance will upset the equilibrium of his steps so that they become irregular. In dressage competitions this is viewed as a serious fault. Only when the horse has achieved such good balance that he can carry himself will he be able to show the true quality of his paces.

Activity

The activity of any of the paces depends upon the flexibility of the hind legs, the essential propulsive force that lifts and thrusts the horse forwards. Many lazy horses will not make the effort unless urged to do so with a schooling whip – although once they accept that they must use themselves more energetically they will become active enough.

Impulsion

Energy, either natural or created by the rider, is the power needed to create and sustain momentum. Energy depends on activity and vice versa: in short, the two should evolve together.

Rhythm

The correct sequence of steps should occur in a regular rhythm; this can be heard easily on a hard surface, but the rider should train himself to *feel* that the steps are regular and rhythmic, too.

Suppleness

The horse cannot perform well if he is stiff, nor will he be comfortable to ride. This subject is explained more fully in Chapter 7, but every rider should realize that the paces will never improve or be really attractive unless the horse is supple.

Variation within the Paces

The variations required within each pace – working, collected, medium and extended – should be developed as a result of a gradual build-up of suppleness, energy and submission, and should not be thought of as unrelated to each other.

THE HORSE'S PACES

Transitions between the Paces

Besides all the variations within the paces there are, of course, the transitions between them; these should be ridden progressively when the horse is learning, but as he becomes more advanced they should be more direct. All transitions should be clear to an onlooker, and the rider must know in his own mind when he has started or finished a change of pace. He must discipline himself and his horse towards being accurate, and should always view any transition as the means of cohesion to work being done.

Analysis of the Paces

The Walk

The best way to find out the feel of a particular horse's natural walk is to allow him to go on a long rein. If he is allowed to walk in a relaxed manner with his neck stretched out and down, the back will have maximum freedom, and the stride should over-track. This means that the hind foot will step beyond the hoofprint left by the forefoot. The horse will feel as if he is really going somewhere, but not in a hurried way, and his back will feel relaxed.

Of course many horses do hurry, and if this is the case, the steps normally feel quick and tense. Tension may also cause the pace to become two-beat instead of four; when this happens the horse 'paces', that is, he swings both legs on the same side forwards at the same time. This is a bad fault, and care must be taken to avoid the tension that causes a two-beat walk.

Some horses on the other hand are very idle and don't want to walk on at all; they will feel reluctant, and it will take ages to get anywhere. This sort should be persuaded very firmly to go forwards by the use of more active leg aids and if necessary a whip.

There are four types of walk:

Medium walk
This is the horse's ordinary walk, although the steps should over-track and he should be on the bit. He must therefore be going forwards from the rider's leg aids, and he should be accepting the aids evenly; his natural neck and head action should not be constrained, however.

Collected walk
The horse is brought more together (this does not mean he is restricted) so the steps become marginally shorter and show more elevation (meaning lift) as a result of improved engagement and impulsion (see Chapter 9).

Extended walk
This is the horse's natural walk going forwards to the maximum degree. The steps should now over-track distinctly, and the neck should stretch forwards with the horse's nose in front of the vertical. He should still be on the bit.

Free walk on a long rein
The horse should be allowed enough rein so that he can lower his head and neck and stretch them forwards and downwards as far as he wants. A light contact should be maintained with his mouth.

There can be problems with this movement if the rider fails to follow the horse as he takes the rein, or if the rein catches the horse in the mouth just as he is going to stretch, and puts him off. If he is taught to take the rein gradually, and as long as the rider gives it gradually, this should not happen.

The reins must obviously be gathered up again after a long rein walk, and this should also be done gradually; any hasty action on the part of the rider will cause the horse to throw up his head or possibly jog as he anticipates the trot.

The Trot

Trots vary enormously, some horses having rhythmic springy strides, others flat, shuffling ones. Improving a poor trot requires considerable skill, and training is so much easier if a horse has a good trot to start with.

A good trot will have a lot of movement, and this can make the horse difficult to sit on. However, with training, and as the horse becomes more supple, this will become easier to master. For riders with any insecurity of position or for those in the process of developing their seat, it is better for the horse if the rider rises to the trot. It is easy to spoil a trot by restricting it in an effort to make it more comfortable, but this will almost certainly be at the expense of the right sort of impulsion.

In all trot work, the steps should be regular (even) and rhythmic, and should spring from one diagonal to the other.

Working trot
The horse should be going forwards willingly, actively and in balance, remaining steadily on the bit.

Collected trot
The horse should be gathered together (see Chapter 9); the steps may be shorter, they should be more elevated, and they should show a clearly defined rhythm.

Medium trot
This is a 'bigger' working trot. It must evolve from collection as it requires a higher degree of engagement (see Chapters 7 and 9) than working trot in order to give it power and lift.

When trying to achieve a bigger trot the rider must guard against the horse falling onto his shoulders. If this happens, the scope of his stride will be inhibited and he will be unable to produce the greater power and impulsion that the medium pace requires.

Extended trot
An even bigger trot, developed from work on the other variations of trot: the extended pace is expressed in tremendous power and maximum ability to cover the ground as the hindquarters lift and drive the horse's mass. The moment of suspension is also extended, so the horse covers maximum ground in the air.

The extended trot presupposes excellent balance, suppleness and acceptance of the aids: it can only be achieved if these criteria are fulfilled.

Problems in trot
Lazy horses are always a problem as they do not want to make any particular effort and their paces can look and feel dull. Rousing them is not easy, but they must be stirred out of their lethargy by active riding, backed up by a whip if needed, and by keeping them interested with a greater variety of exercises.

Excitable horses are often more difficult and will need a great deal of patience and time before their work becomes established.

Some of the biggest problems in trot arise because horses are stiff or do not accept their rider's aids properly; lack of rhythm and irregularity in the stride in particular are caused by these mistakes.

Some horses learn to 'hop', or to go crooked: if these evasions are continually allowed they can be very hard indeed to correct and the paces will be seriously impaired; great care should therefore be taken never to allow such things to start.

Another common evasion is that of not going forwards properly, but instead hanging back. This kind of trot, often called a 'dwelling' trot, may feel quite good as it often has considerable lift. Unfortunately this is not the result of impulsion, but of insufficient desire to move forwards, and so it cannot be considered a good quality pace.

The Canter

A good canter is one which is naturally well balanced and has a significant moment of suspension between strides; it is a great advantage if a horse is good in this pace. A poor canter is the hardest pace for the rider to improve; it is difficult even for an expert, but for those who may lack in strength of seat it is very hard indeed to achieve the engagement needed to make improvement. A canter is so often on the forehand, and when it is the horse finds it easy to lean on his rider's hands or to pull. However, pulling back or trying to raise his head with the hands alone is not the answer; to improve the canter the hindquarters must be brought under the horse's body to lift his forehand, and this can only be done by strong use of the seat and leg aids, combined with the half-halt (see Chapter 7).

Working canter
The canter should be balanced, well engaged (see Chapter 7) and should move actively forwards. The horse should be round in his outline and accepting the aids.

Collected canter
The strides are shorter and more bouncy. The horse feels very together and as though he is travelling 'uphill' – meaning that he carries his weight on his quarters so his shoulders are free – but his outline should always be round, not hollow.

Medium canter
This evolves from collection, so the forehand remains light. The strides are bigger and more above the ground than in the working or collected canters.

Extended canter
A bigger edition of the medium canter with even more suspension so that the horse covers considerable ground in the air.

Problems in canter
There are many problems that can occur in canter. Lack of balance is probably the main one, but loss or lack of sufficient energy is certainly another. This causes the horse to labour, which can result in losing the three-beat sequence of steps. This is a bad fault and riders must try to develop a feel for any loss of impulsion which may produce a four-beat canter.

When working on a circle, the horse will normally be required to canter with his inside foreleg leading: this term is used because the action of the inside foreleg is slightly in front of the other. The aids for this are as follows: the rider should sit straight and look up; he controls the speed with the outside rein, flexes the horse to the inside with the inside rein, warns the horse which leg he is to canter on by moving his own outside leg behind the girth, and then asks for canter by using the inside leg.

If the horse strikes off correctly the rider should feel this, or may even be able to see the horse's inside shoulder coming forwards. It is very important that he learns to recognize this feel, because if he is unsure, the horse may well become confused himself and achieving the correct strike-off will become a problem. Once the horse has started off on the wrong leg a few times and been repeatedly checked and restarted, he will get fed up and will end up deciding for himself, thus causing his rider great difficulty.

Even after a correct strike-off the horse may sometimes lose his balance and as a result will change leg either behind or in front (in other words, not a true change, in which both change). This is called 'being disunited', and can be recognized because the pace takes on a rolling motion and becomes most uncomfortable. The horse should be brought to trot, rebalanced, and the canter begun again.

Crookedness is another common problem. For the correction see Chapter 7.

The Gallop

Being able to show a good gallop in a showing class is very important, and so is being able to sustain one, in balance, when riding across country.

The sequence of footfalls in gallop is actually four-beat, as in walk; however, this is of no particular significance, it is just something every rider should know as a matter of interest. Besides, in gallop there is generally little chance to think about footfalls: the question of control is far more important.

Whether going across country, or as part of his individual 'show' in a showing class, the horse should not be allowed to gallop as fast as he wants to go, but must allow his rider to regulate the speed, as at any other pace. If he gets onto his forehand he will not be able either to control himself or to operate safely, so this should not be allowed to happen.

Being able to control the gallop easily comes from progressive schooling, so that at each stage the rider remains in charge. The transitions from canter to gallop and back into canter should be practised to make sure that the horse waits for his instructions and does what he is told.

Conformation

The importance of conformation has already been mentioned. The correct build of the horse does affect his paces, but although everyone wants a well made horse which moves well there are certainly no rules, and some of the most unlikely looking animals move well, and vice versa.

Movement

When assessing the horse's paces it is more useful to see them from the side than from in front or behind. Of course the latter aspect will show whether the horse moves straight, but only from the side can the freedom of the shoulders, the scope of the stride and the activity of the hind legs really be assessed.

Scope is vital to the horse's ability to perform well, whatever the discipline, so any limitations are best avoided. Dishing does not really constitute a handicap

THE HORSE'S PACES

Horse showing a concave or 'hollow' outline

A 'round' outline. However, the horse's nose is a little behind the vertical, which is incorrect.

because scope depends on shoulder movement, but it is often unsightly and, as has already been mentioned, is frowned upon in the show ring.

Temperament

A horse's temperament has a considerable effect on his paces. For example an idle horse will offer problems for the rider because he will not show off his paces to best advantage; while tension in the horse can result in lack of rhythm, uneven steps, jogging in walk, breaks of pace, resistance and all manner of other evasions which affect the purity of the steps.

Outline

Unless the horse works in the correct shape all his paces will suffer. A correct outline is one in which he moves with his head flexed at the poll, his neck arched and his back rounded with a lowered croup. This means his hindquarters are positioned further underneath his body, so the energy they generate is transmitted upwards through his frame to take him forwards. Providing he also has muscular suppleness this outline will enable him to work most effectively, with maximum spring in his paces.

CHAPTER 7
Straightness, Balance, Suppleness and Submission

Straightness

What to Look For

A horse should be viewed both from in front and from behind to assess whether it is straight. From in front the observer ascertains the action of the forelegs: some horses move wide, that is to say the distance between their forefeet, on the move, is wider than the width of the chest. This is usually due to conformation and not training, so there is little that can be done about it. Some people do not like the look of this action, but apart from appearance it is of no disadvantage except in a show class.

Toes that turn in are unattractive in my opinion, and tend to make the horse move with his elbows out; this is never a good thing as it can weaken the function of those joints. Also, the horse may be more inclined to trip.

Dishing with one or both forelegs can be quite ugly and may affect the joints or the way the hoof comes to the ground. It is not really desirable, although from a training point of view dishing often affects performance less than horses which move with their toes turned in.

Knee action does not cause any training problems that I am aware of, and in many ways the flexibility is an advantage.

Looking at the horse from behind, the hind legs should be straight, that is the hocks should not point towards each other; they should stand underneath the hindquarters, and not be built out behind them. When the horse moves, his hind feet should follow exactly in the tracks of the forefeet; the joints should flex so that there is no dragging of the toes.

Cow hocks are hocks that turn inwards and are a sign of weakness because they may affect the driving power of the hindquarters. The toes will turn out as well, so that in effect all the joints are affected.

It is also important to look at the horse's whole frame from behind in order to see whether the hips are level, and whether the spine appears to be straight. If there is a physiological problem, no amount of training will put it right.

What it Feels Like

When riding, the rider must be sensitive enough in his seat to feel whether his horse is equal. He must ask himself whether the horse feels stronger on one side of his back than he does on the other, which may indicate uneven development of the back muscles. This is a common problem, as many riders sit lop-sided and thus are a direct cause of this happening.

STRAIGHTNESS AND BALANCE

This fault is frequently seen: the hind feet are not following in the tracks of the forefeet and the head and neck are not aligned.

Although this horse is on a curve his hind feet are following in the tracks of the forefeet.

The right- or left-handedness of the rider can affect the straightness of the horse, too. Whether or not the horse is born with a similar tendency is debatable, but because he is led from the left-hand side he may become one-sided for this reason. Whatever the cause, most horses will bend to one direction more easily than to the other, which indicates uneven muscle development. When ridden, the horse needs constant correction to his length in order to keep all parts of his frame in alignment with each other. The forehand is especially awkward because the neck is so flexible; so often the horse's head and neck are bent one way while his shoulders are travelling in the other. Constant correction of the head, neck and shoulders are necessary to maintain straightness.

The body and hindquarters should be controlled by the rider's legs so that the horse's weight does not swing about, which will make him unbalanced and difficult to steer. Making the horse go forwards is the best straightening exercise of all, as there is less opportunity for him to deviate from the line he is on. This is most easily done in trot: in walk he has more time to wriggle around.

The canter especially produces a great deal of crookedness because, due to the horse's length, the rider is often unaware of what the hindquarters are doing. In a school the horse will generally put his quarters inwards; as he is wider at the rear end than at the front he may feel cramped with them on the track. To help him, the rider should bring the forehand a little away from the side of the school, which will bring it in line with the hindquarters. This is called riding with the 'shoulders fore', or in shoulder-in position (see Chapter 9).

When trying to ride the horse straight the rider should aim at an object, keeping it in sight between his horse's ears. In this way it is more obvious when crookedness occurs, and it can be corrected quickly. Straightness is often a rider problem: if the aids are weak, or if the horse is not really going forwards, then he is more likely to wobble off a designated line. Also, any unevenness of the aids may allow a crookedness to develop. In short, riders who sit badly themselves cannot expect their horse to go straight!

The importance of being able to go straight is not simply a matter of control, but also because the horse needs to be able to see where he is going, which he cannot do if his head is pulled to one side.

Balance

What to Look For

To assess if a horse is balanced the rider should observe how easily he performs. Does he accomplish what he is asked to do

This horse is clearly 'on his forehand': the weight is being taken by the shoulders.

STRAIGHTNESS AND BALANCE

with minimum effort, or does he fall about and struggle? Most of the horse's weight is naturally in his forehand, and with the additional burden of a rider, inevitably this is accentuated. Thus throughout his ridden life the horse's balance has to be organized for him by his rider, who must constantly adjust it so that it is taken evenly by each of his limbs. Because in his natural way of going it is chiefly on the forelegs, so it is plain therefore that the hind legs must be persuaded to take more of an equal share. This is done by regulating speed and rhythm so as to achieve a gradual increase in the engagement of the hind legs. By doing this the croup will lower, allowing the hindquarters to come further beneath the horse so that they can take more weight and therefore lighten the forehand.

What it Feels Like

It is essential for the rider to learn to recognize whether or not the horse is balanced. If the horse is wandering about, or his shoulders are falling in or out on corners, or his hindquarters are swinging around, he is not balanced. Also, if he feels heavy in front or leans on the rider's hands, if he slips and slides around or gets his head in the air, again, he is not balanced. There are many other such moments to recognize, but the important thing is for the rider to be aware that the horse cannot do what he, the rider, wants unless it is balanced.

The Half-halt

The most useful exercise for the creation or correction of balance is the half-halt. In its simplest form it is merely a steadying aid which the rider can use when the horse is trying to go too fast – though when I say 'steadying' the rider should appreciate that he must still use his seat and legs to keep the horse going forwards as he restrains with his hands. To define it more exactly, the half-halt is the combined use of the seat, legs and hands of the rider which coordinate so exactly that their action results in a momentary collection of the pace in order to increase the engagement of the hindquarters. This moment of collection should not only correct and improve balance, it will also increase the horse's attention to the aids. If all this happens as it should, the horse will be in a better position to go forwards more efficiently.

Activity and Engagement

Unless the horse responds actively to his rider's leg aids, his hindquarters will not engage as they should. The rider knows when he has sufficient activity because the horse should feel as if it is taking him along with the minimum of effort from himself, and if he gives an aid, it should respond instantly, indicating that not only is it active physically, it is also mentally alert.

The joints of the horse's hind legs should flex fully, without snatching, and not in a sluggish fashion. They should feel as if they are pushing his body forwards and upwards, and they should create a feeling that he is bursting with life and vigour. The horse should feel that he has the sort of mobility that enables him to do his work with ease.

Impulsion

Good balance cannot evolve without impulsion: the energy provided by the

STRAIGHTNESS AND BALANCE

Rider 'giving the rein' to test the balance. The horse falls onto his forehand.

When the rider 'gives the rein' this time, the horse remains in balance.

STRAIGHTNESS AND BALANCE

hindquarters that gives momentum to the paces. First of all the horse must be active, his hindquarters must engage, and only then can more energy be asked for. This must then necessarily be controlled by the rider's hands, the amount regulated depending on each situation, and then used to accomplish whatever the rider wishes to do.

Only from an ability to contain energy will the rider be able to use it effectively. For example, he will need more if jumping a five-foot fence, but far less at a lower height. On the flat, more is needed for an extended trot than for working, and so on.

When the horse is made to be more impulsive he may become strong, but he must not be allowed to pull or lean on his rider's hands. For this reason he must also learn self-carriage.

Self-carriage

The rider will ultimately know when his horse is balanced if it can carry itself without being supported by the reins. This does not mean riding on a loose rein. What it does mean is that the horse, being active, engaged and impulsive, will not fall on his head or gallop off when the reins are momentarily released, or if the contact is lightened.

The best exercise to achieve this result is the giving and re-taking of the reins, when the rider releases the contact he has on the reins, either one rein at a time, or both, depending on his desire at the time. The contact should be released carefully, and after a stride or two, regained equally carefully, and all the while this is being done the horse should not grab the bit, nor alter his position, nor break the pace. The rider must retain his own position, and should achieve the giving and re-taking by simply stretching his arm or arms. This action should not be used repeatedly because it is desirable to maintain a steady, light contact with the horse's mouth; but it is invaluable as a test of the horse's balance.

Suppleness

What to Look For

Without suppleness the horse will look rigid in his work and he will appear to find it difficult. His mouth will look set and dry, and he will not flex at the poll. His body will not curve easily on corners or circles, and his hind legs may trail out behind him. His action may well be affected, appearing jerky or stilted.

A supple horse and rider will appear moulded together, displaying an ease of performance that is pleasant to watch.

What it Feels Like

Longitudinal suppleness is the flexibility that the horse shows in its ability to be round through its neck and back. It can only come about from engagement of the hindquarters, suppleness of the back muscles and flexion by the poll and lower jaw. The horse's back should then be able to move elastically under the rider, which will feel comfortable to sit on. When the horse is stiff in his back he will hold himself rigidly, or will even hollow his back away from the rider; this causes jarring in his paces and makes him very difficult to sit on. It is also bad for him because in hollowing in this way he may actually damage his back muscles.

Lateral suppleness is the ability of the horse's body to curve round his rider's

STRAIGHTNESS AND BALANCE

inside leg, giving him bend; this can only occur if the shoulders and hindquarters are sufficiently flexible. The rider will feel if his horse is bending, from the yield that he obtains when his inside leg closes against its side.

Suppleness can only come about from the routine exercise of body muscle, which must have an overall gradual development.

The movement of the horse, his paces and his entire training can only be enhanced by the quality of suppleness. All the work in the school is designed to achieve this (as long as the movements are ridden properly), and the purpose of all the exercises such as shoulder-in and half-pass, travers and renvers, is to increase suppling and manoeuvrability (see Chapter 9).

Submission

What to Look For

A horse which is *not* submissive to his rider will show visible resistance by opening his mouth, throwing his head around, swinging his hind-quarters or using his bodyweight to go where he wants to go. Some will kick at the leg aids, swish their tails or may be heard to grind their teeth. Others will hang their tongue out of their mouth, tilt their head or overbend continually.

These evasions may be caused by all manner of contingencies, such as an unsuitable bit (too large, too small or too severe), roughly applied aids or perhaps an inconsiderate demand on the part of the rider – what the horse is being asked

Evasion by overbending.

STRAIGHTNESS AND BALANCE

Resistance to the bit as indicated by the horse's open mouth.

The horse is submitting to pressure from the reins but his head carriage is too low and the hindquarters are insufficiently 'engaged'.

STRAIGHTNESS AND BALANCE

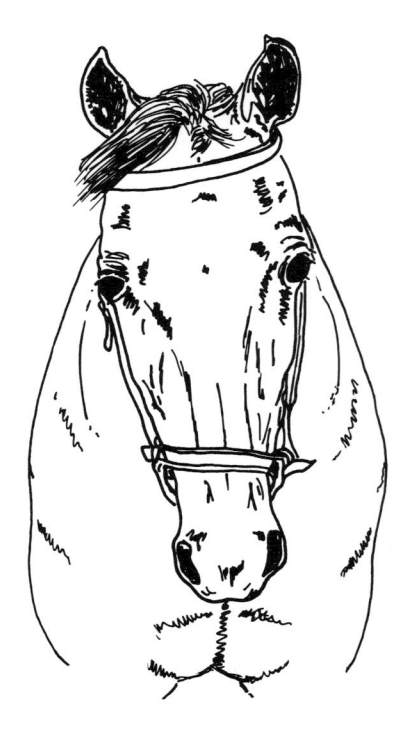

Head tilting is an evasion.

This horse is clearly unhappy — his jaw is crossed and his tongue out.

may be beyond his capacity, or he may not have understood.

Resistance is not only ugly, it also results in a bad performance, so the rider must always make his intentions clear and take the blame when things go wrong.

A submissive horse does what his rider wants at the time because he is able and willing. He should not be coerced into such a state but should be a willing partner.

What you Should Feel

A sensitive rider will know instantly if his horse is reluctant to do what he wants or actively resists it. Opposition to an exercise should be analyzed to determine the reason, but every rider must double check his initial question. The entire training of the horse depends on him being made to understand what the aids mean, and on his acceptance of them.

Once the horse fully comprehends the meaning of the leg aids he must be asked to accept the bit also. The rider may feel this acceptance by the way the horse yields to the contact he has with his mouth via the reins. Although there is much natural sensitivity around and in the mouth and this should never be abused by rough handling, sensitivity to a contact with the rider through the reins must be aroused by the feel-and-ease action of the rider's fingers. For this reason it is pointless to ride with no contact at all, and in fact this *can* be more unpleasant for the horse because if and when the rein *is* taken up, his mouth

STRAIGHTNESS AND BALANCE

generally receives a meaningless jerk.

Contact is often resisted quite forcibly before the horse will 'give' to it, but if the rider backs off from the process he will never achieve the desired result. When the horse does resist pressure, the rider should move the bit gently with an alternate pressure until the horse submits, at which point the pressure must be immediately eased.

Dealing with Evasions

As has already been explained, there are many ways in which the horse will try to avoid being submissive. He does so because sometimes he does not want to make the effort, or it may be painful to him; equally he may be feeling tired, or over-excited or anxious. Whatever the reason, the rider should firmly but patiently make the necessary correction.

There may also be occasions when the horse is downright nappy and refuses outright to do what he is told, and then the rider must take an instant and positive attitude. He should send the horse forwards in any way he can, or failing that, turn it in a circle; in this way the horse is prevented from taking the initiative, giving the rider a better chance to regain the upper hand.

In all matters of obedience the question must be clear, and when the horse gives the right answer he must be rewarded.

Control

Control over the horse will only be gained from a true acceptance of the rider's aids, therefore it is of utmost importance to get it right. Some riders under-control their horses by giving them insufficient instructions; others overdo it, which is restrictive. Every rider must assess his own attitude, and his ability to gain the control required for the movement or activity he wants to achieve.

CHAPTER 8
School Movements and Exercises

It is important that the horse's basic training takes place in a proper school because not only is it easier for horse and rider to concentrate, but the movements to be executed only develop the horse in the right way if they are ridden with accuracy. The schooling area to be used should measure either 20 x 40m or 20 x 60m.

Many riders are put off by the sight of school figures, but study of the diagrams is necessary if they are to be executed properly. Before attempting to ride any movement, the rider should consider the following sequence of events, a pattern he might well be advised to observe:

1. He decides what exercise is to be tried.
2. He warns the horse by asking for increased attention to the aids.
3. He gives the aid.
4. The horse responds.
5. The rider judges the result of the horse's response.
6. He makes a correction if required or begins the exercise again.
7. He rewards the horse.

During all movements the rider must continually assess his horse's state of mind, and ask himself:

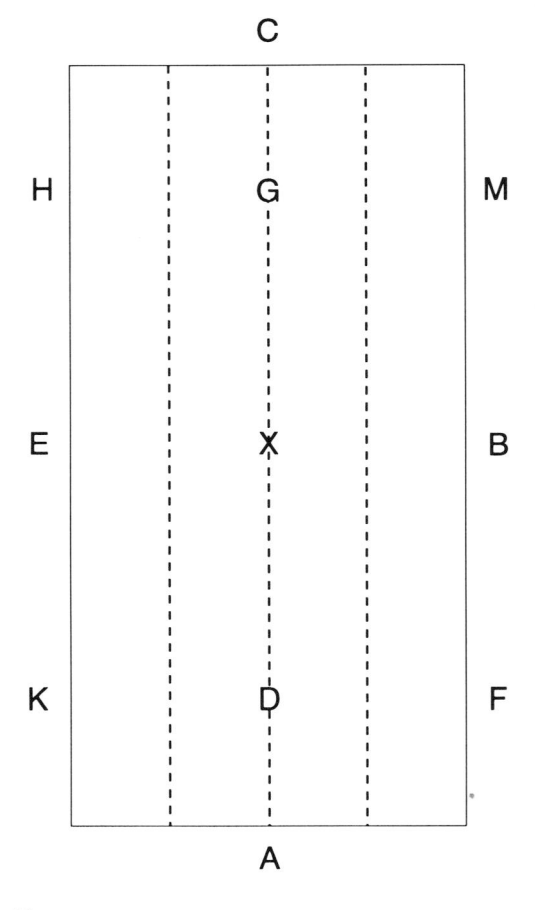

Dressage arena – novice size.

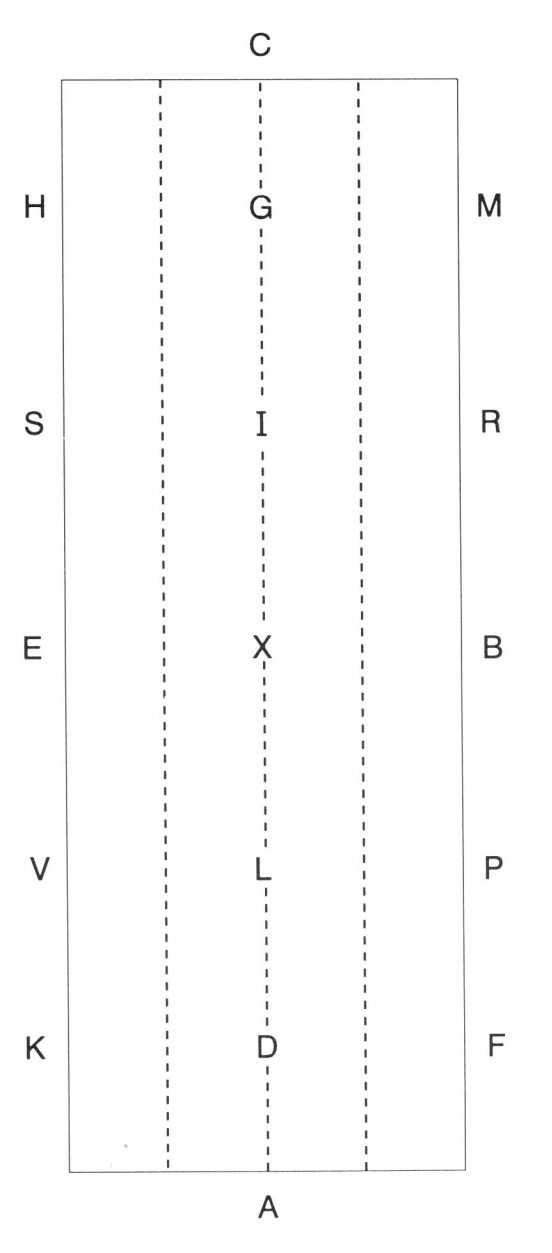

SCHOOL MOVEMENTS AND EXERCISES

- Is the horse listening to the aids?
- Does he understand the aids?
- Can he do what he is being asked?
- Is he mentally and physically relaxed?
- Was he properly prepared?

Self-discipline is hard but it is essential to success, and accurate riding of the figures is important. Sloppy riding will be reflected in a poor end result.

Riding the Arena

Every school of the dimensions given above is composed of four sides and four corners, and each one of these must be ridden properly. On the sides the horse should be straight, and in the corners he should be curved to the line he is following. A novice horse will adopt less of a curve than a more advanced horse (see diagrams). Although the rider will be

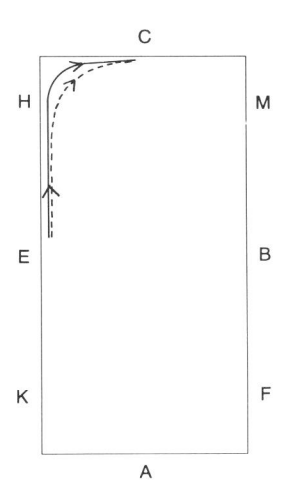

Dressage arena – advanced size.

Cornering for novice and advanced horses.

SCHOOL MOVEMENTS AND EXERCISES

asking the horse to be straight, then to bend, then be straight again and so on, there should be no abruptness involved; the aim overall should be fluidity of movement.

When working in a school the horse should be worked equally on both reins so that he does not become one-sided (stiffer on one rein than the other). He can be asked to change the rein in various ways: for example, by crossing the school on a diagonal line from one quarter marker to another, when he should adopt appropriate curves at each end of the line, and remain straight in between; the rider should always keep his eye on the marker to which he is heading. Alternatively his rider might change the rein by riding up the centre line; by crossing the school at the half markers; or by riding half circles within a circle.

Circles

These may be of varying sizes and can be ridden in various places in the school. On a circle the horse should be curved to the

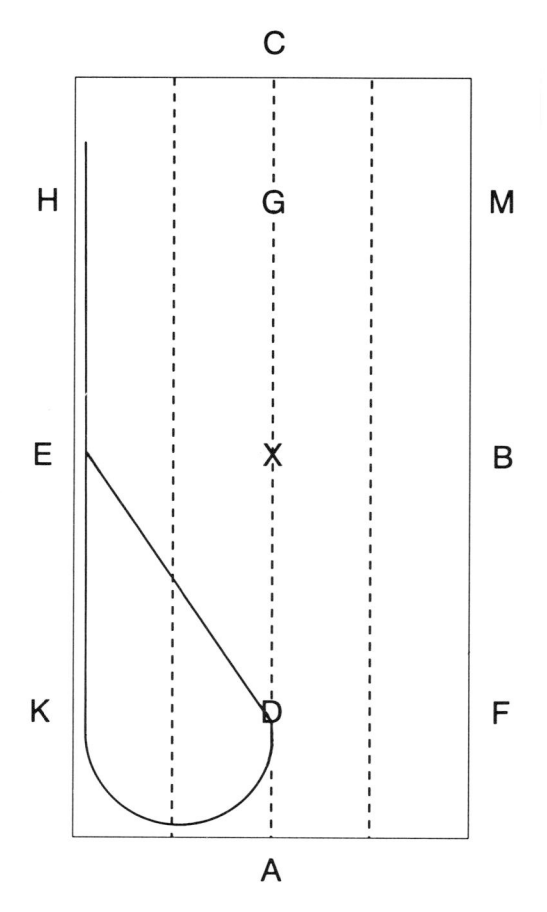

Half circle, returning to the track at E.

Finishing a circle showing the curve that the horse has taken.

SCHOOL MOVEMENTS AND EXERCISES

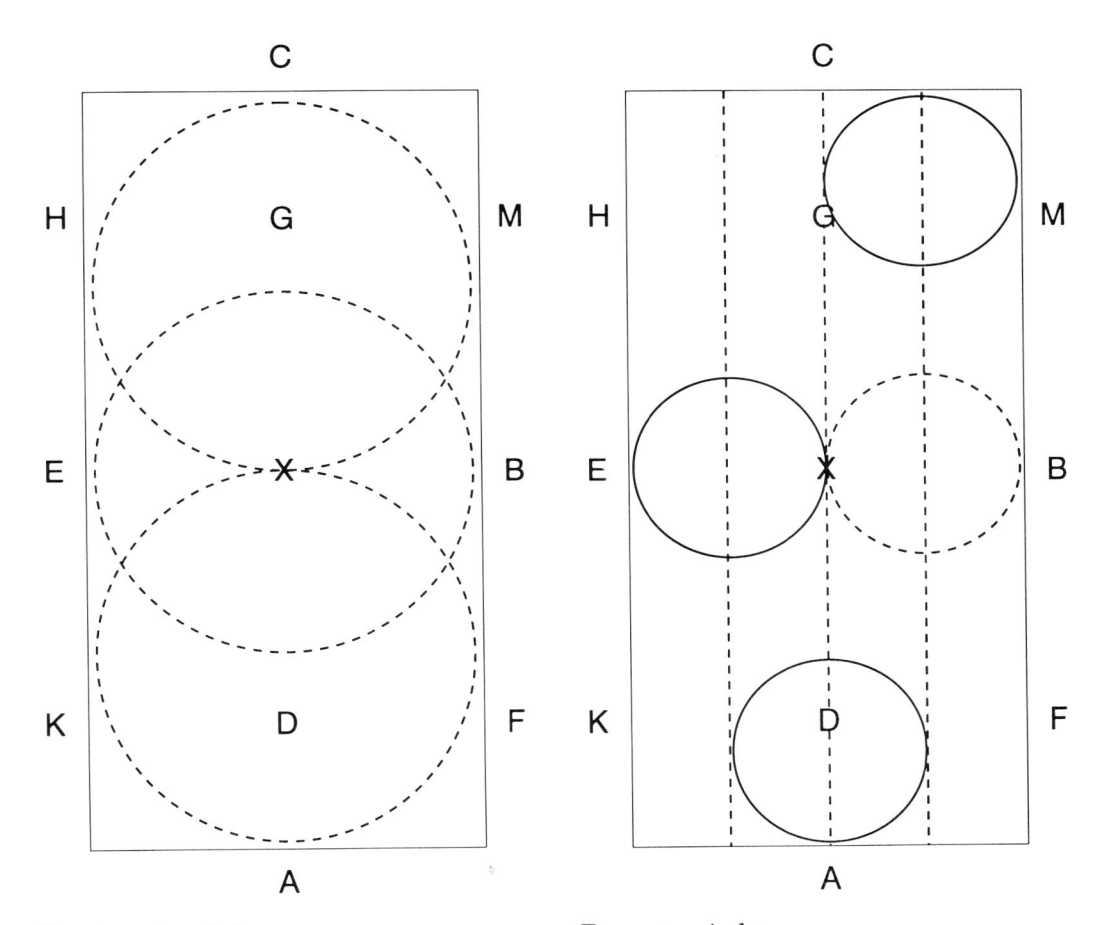

Twenty-metre circles.

Ten-metre circles.

same degree as the circumference of that particular circle; thus on a 20m circle the curve through his body will be less than on a 10m circle. The rider should warn his horse of the degree of the bend required before he starts the circle by positioning the horse's forehand (see Chapter 9), and by taking a flexion to the inside.

Circles should be round and not lemon-shaped, and in the case of figures of eight the circles should match each other in size and therefore bend.

The horse should not be allowed to lean in (like a motor bike) against his rider's inside leg, nor should he continually pull to the outside. His neck bend should not be greater than the bend in the rest of his body, and his head should not tilt. Should either situation arise the rider should re-assess his aids: most problems occur because the inside leg aid is too weak; also it may not be coordinating well enough with the outside rein which should be in control of the horse's speed and the size of the circle. Other problems occur when the rider uses the inside rein too strongly; this

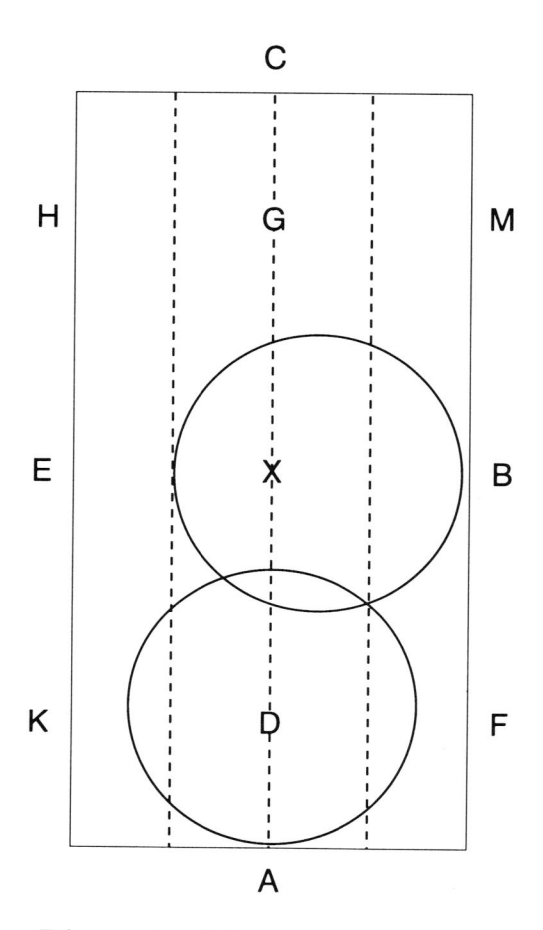

SCHOOL MOVEMENTS AND EXERCISES

Loops and Serpentines

Other useful exercises include loops of 3 or 5m from the track, and serpentines across the school (see diagrams). These should all adopt the appropriate curve. Accuracy is important because any discrepancy may cause difficulty for the horse, so the rider must think ahead.

All exercises need planning, and the rider must have a clear idea of where he is going. This is common sense, of course, but it is surprising how often I see horses

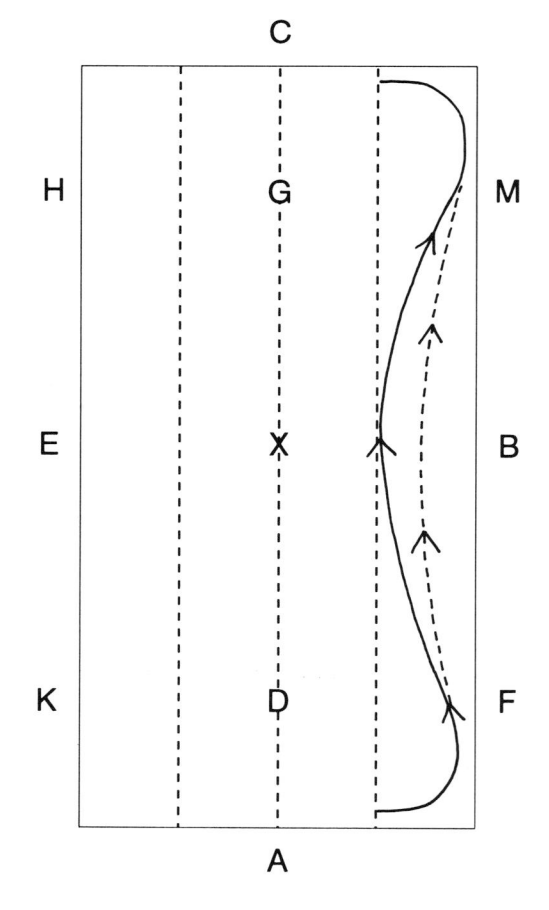

Fifteen-metre circles.

will often restrict the freedom of the paces and inhibit forward movement.

As and when the horse's training demands, circles of a smaller size can be ridden, but these should retain the qualities of balance, suppleness and self-carriage: only if these are present can the other essentials such as rhythm and regularity of the steps be maintained. Smaller circles or half-circles also require varying degrees of collection (see Chapter 9) and cannot be ridden otherwise.

Three- and five-metre loops.

SCHOOL MOVEMENTS AND EXERCISES

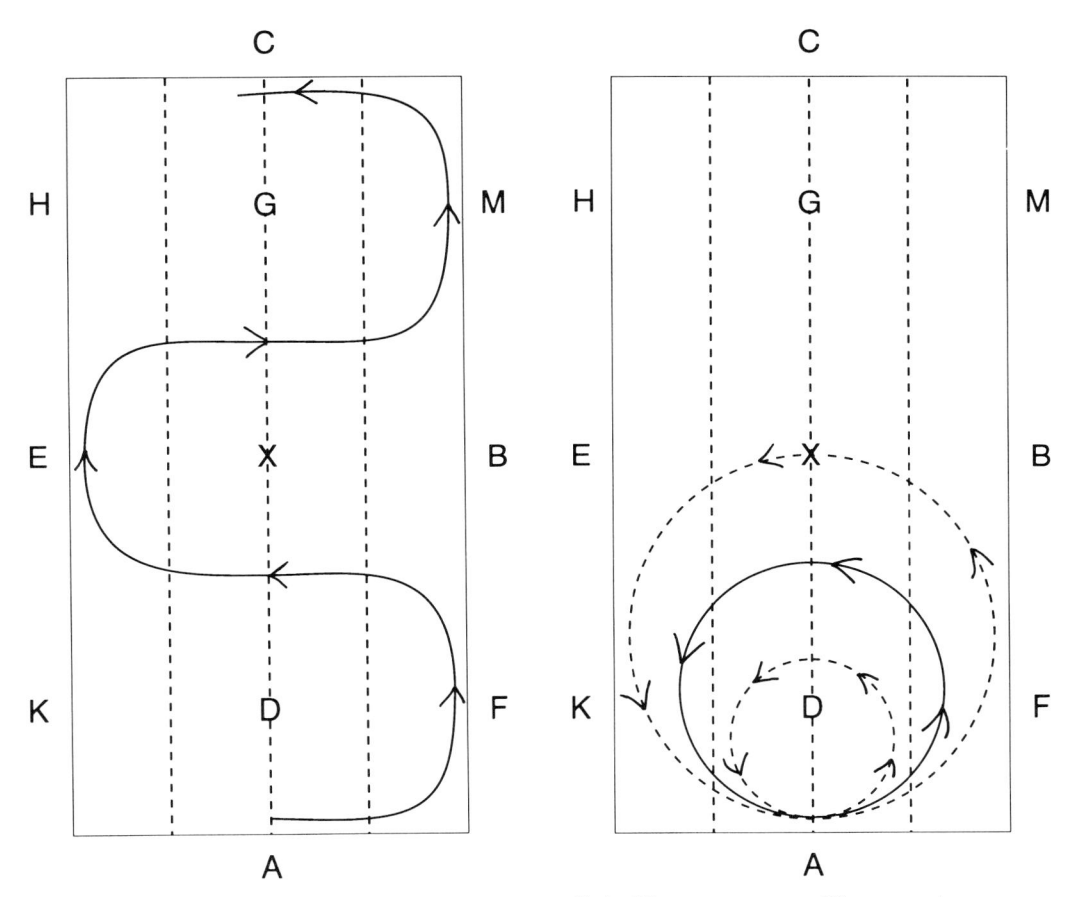

Three-loop serpentine.

Spiralling on twenty-, fifteen- and ten-metre circles.

getting themselves into a tangle because their riders are indecisive or vague!

Riding a sequence of circles spiralling in or out is an invaluable exercise for improving the horse's attention, suppleness and balance. The rider must ride accurately, beginning each new circle at the same marker, otherwise the benefit is lost.

Most of the exercises can be ridden at all three paces, but the rider should only consider a faster pace when the current one has been satisfactorily mastered.

Another exercise which is extremely beneficial is riding a square, in particular with regard to the rider learning more exact control. The square should not be too small as the exercise entails the aids being well co-ordinated, an ability which at first may be lacking. The rider turns the horse at each corner by means of a small pirouette (see Chapter 9) of about two steps, thus bringing the horse onto the new line. In order to control the forehand, a shoulder-in position is then needed (Chapter 9). From these closely related

SCHOOL MOVEMENTS AND EXERCISES

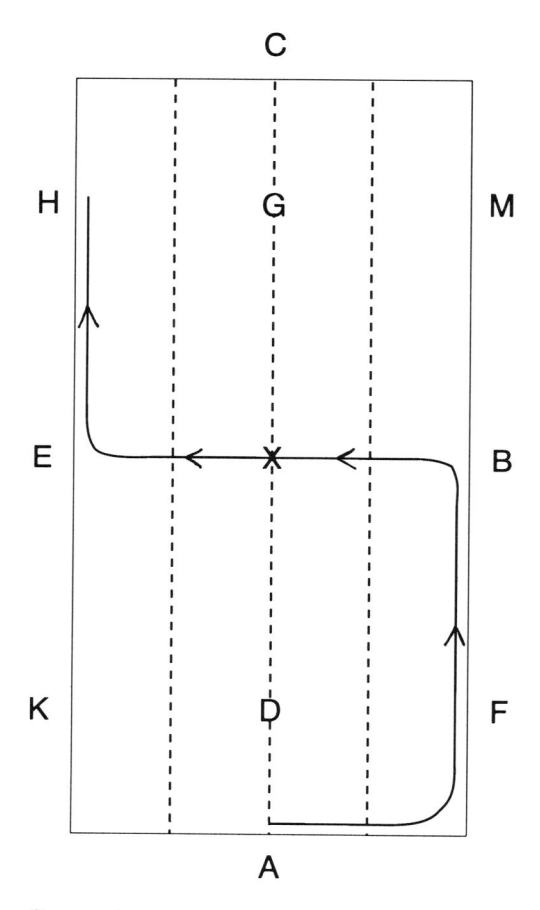

Square turns.

be part of the work. Apart from small circles or loops and serpentines which demand collection, variations may be used in many of the school exercises. The purpose is to improve suppleness and response to the aids, and to prepare the horse for extensions.

The amount of variation to expect can be as little as a small difference within the working pace. The important point is that the horse should be able to maintain his balance and rhythm, and that he enlarges and reduces his steps smoothly and without resistance. Unless the hindquarters are engaged and the horse accepts the aids this will not happen.

In trot the rider may sit or rise, depending on his security in the saddle, but he must remember that shifting his weight may upset the horse's equilibrium.

It is generally best to start pace variations on the long side of the school, because straightness is essential to the correct result. Also, the novice horse will find it easier to hold his balance on the long side. As training progresses, variations on a circle or round corners should be incorporated, with great care taken to maintain balance.

aids the rider obtains greater control; it also teaches him to feel evasions when they occur and to deal with them quickly.

The square should be ridden mainly in walk and canter because in trot the pirouette is not practised; although it can be attempted in trot by riding the corners as tighter turns than normal.

Pace Variation

In all paces, variation of the stride should

Accuracy

Developing accuracy is important but the quality of the horse's way of going is more so, certainly to begin with. As time goes on, the horse's increased acceptance to the aids will enable the rider to take the control he needs to be more precise.

Preparation

The aids for all movements differ very

SCHOOL MOVEMENTS AND EXERCISES

little, as each hand and leg has its own job to do (see Chapter 4). The important thing to remember is to give the horse sufficient warning before expecting it to carry out an instruction, by making certain that it is listening to the aids. Having given a warning – which may included preparing for a change in bend – the rider should expect the horse to be alert, but it will need time to reorganize itself, so the actual carrying out of the instruction can only happen gradually.

Having given his aid, the rider cannot sit back and do nothing, but must 'talk' his horse through every step of the excercise.

Watching

Watching the experts is always worthwhile. Consider arranging to visit a dressage trainer to watch him or her working his horses, or teaching a pupil, in order to see exactly how the school movements should be ridden. Some trainers may not be willing to allow outsiders to watch what they are doing, but others will be only too pleased to welcome a newcomer. A phone call with a polite request is always worth trying.

Alternatively you should go to a show to watch tests being ridden. Different movements are required at each level and this may be discovered by buying a book of tests from the Dressage Department of the British Horse Society. Choose the level you are interested in and go and watch that. It will soon be apparent who is riding accurately and who is more slapdash.

The Importance of Feel

With a clear picture in your mind of the various movements it should be possible to develop a feel for them. Feeling for loss of, or lack of balance should be of first concern, because none of the movements can be ridden well if the horse cannot maintain good balance. Furthermore a horse may offer resistance at any moment – when he is asked to bend, or when he is asked to come more on to the aids – and it is up to the rider to recognize the resistance and know what to do about it. For example, if the horse tries to cut the corners or lean in on a circle, the rider should realize instantly and use his aids, especially his inside leg, more effectively. If the bend does not improve, the aids have not been sufficiently strong.

Sometimes a rider's mental conception of a movement or an exercise is unclear and he simply cannot picture where he wants to go. In this case it may help to draw an arena on a sheet of paper and then draw the movement that is puzzling him. When he next rides, his mind may then give better instructions to his body.

By concentrating the mind, the body gradually gains the right feel for the various exercises, and then they should be more easily retained. This does not always happen, however, and a rider may feel very frustrated if he was sure he had grasped something, only to lose it again. But this often happens in training, mainly because of the inconsistencies in the human character, combined with the horse's own feelings at the time. It is hard not to become annoyed in these circumstances – but every rider suffers frustration at some time or another, and has to learn to control his emotions.

Every new movement ridden will present its own problems, and only time and practice will give the rider the feel he wants.

SCHOOL MOVEMENTS AND EXERCISES

Dealing with Problems

Some movements cause more difficulty than others. Generally this is because the rider has not worked out exactly where to go in the arena, although in addition the horse may be anxious because he is being asked to leave the security of the track. This feeling of security is not always understood by the rider, who becomes annoyed when the horse is reluctant to leave it. So much of the work is done by the fence or wall of the school that, without realizing it, both rider and horse come to rely on it. And because the horse starts to go round automatically the rider becomes complacent, believing he is in control; but when the time comes to move out from the track, both are at a loss.

The answer to this difficulty is for the rider to be more aware of the control he has (or otherwise), and for him to ensure that he asks the horse to move about the arena, and doesn't let him become stuck to the track as if on a merry-go-round.

Riding up the centre line seems to cause a great deal of trouble for many riders. Usually the turn onto it initiates the problem because it is accomplished either too early or too late (see diagram). It is important always to look ahead, and the rider should have planned where he wants to go long before the actual turn. At the point of the turn he must look up the line towards C or A, whichever it may be, but he must also think about positioning the horse in such a way that the marker which is behind him as he turns is directly behind the horse's tail. So many riders fail to do this and find themselves at an oblique angle.

I am often told that such and such a horse hots up when turning onto the centre line, or that another becomes completely dead to the aids – but whether they die or hot up has to be mainly due to the rider! I would accept that the horse anticipates the halt or whatever else he may be required to do on the centre line, but for the temperament problems there can be no other real reason.

In a competition situation, rider nerves undoubtedly affect the way the aids are given, and the horse can also sense a difference to what he knows as 'normal', but this can be overcome with experience. Nerves can certainly weaken the effect of the aids and the strength of the rider's seat, and horses also suffer from nerves, though not in quite the same way as humans. A rider may anticipate ignominious defeat due to his own foolishness; the horse is merely keyed up by the general activity of a competition or possibly also by an unpleasant experience he has had previously.

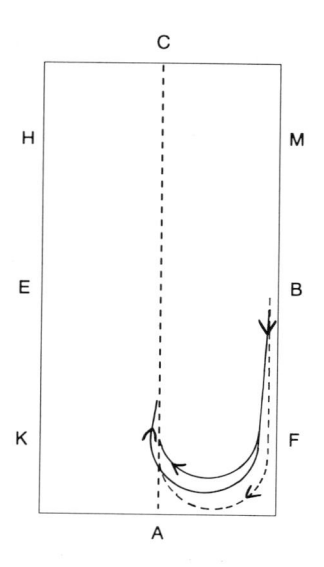

Turning up the centre.

SCHOOL MOVEMENTS AND EXERCISES

Maintaining Impulsion

There is little doubt that tension in the rider may affect his ability to influence the horse in the right way, but being passive is just as ineffectual.

Too much tension results in stiffness which may cause the rider's limbs to act rigidly. Learning to relax and yet be able to use the muscles strongly is an art that has to be learned and takes much practice; but until it is, it will be hard either to create or to maintain impulsion in the horse.

Although it is good to be relaxed in order to ride well, if a rider is *too* relaxed the messages he gives the horse may be vague or woolly; and if this is so, his reactions may be vague also.

Once impulsion is lost, movements become very difficult to ride; nor do they have any value, either. With the right amount of energy all the work will seem easier.

Cantering on the Wrong Leg

This is a very common mistake which, if allowed to develop, presents long-term difficulties. Horses very quickly become one-sided and stiff if allowed always to lead on their favourite leg. In this respect I cannot stress enough how important it is for the rider to be able to tell which leg the horse is about to strike off with: by the time he has actually done it, it is too late!

The answer to this problem is in the development of feel which, if it is not natural, must evolve from a secure, deep seat and firm concentration. Some horses are very persistent, and unless they are strongly ridden will continue to choose the leg they prefer. The best place in the school to get a result is going into a short side. If the aid is given at the preceding quarter marker, by the time the message has reached the horse he will be on the corner so his natural inclination will be to balance himself by leading with his inside foreleg. If this method fails, it may become necessary to off-balance the horse temporarily by bending him to the outside. This also serves to restrict the freedom of the outside shoulder which prevents him choosing that lead.

If there is still a problem, a pole may be placed in the corner. The horse should be trotted up to it, but just beforehand he should be asked to canter. It is then important to keep him going. I have seldom known this method to fail, and once the horse becomes accustomed to cantering on his least favourite leg, the pole can be removed.

Anticipation

There will be many times in training when the horse will anticipate what he thinks he is going to be asked. His memory of the work he has learned will trigger an early response as he associates it with various places in the school. However, although he must learn to obey his rider and to listen to what he is being asked, the rider should not be impatient with these reactions as they indicate a willingness to please.

Also, a horse can become hyper-sensitive to his rider's wishes so that any slight movement may be interpreted as an aid; so the rider must have good control of his actions.

CHAPTER 9

Further Schooling on the Flat

Once the horse has learned the basics (see Chapters 6, 7 and 8), other exercises are introduced for the purpose of increasing obedience and suppleness and achieving a higher degree of agility. Two exercises useful to the rider in obtaining an increased response to the leg aids are the turn on the forehand and the leg-yield.

Turn on the Forehand

This term, I feel, implies that the horse should be allowed to put weight onto his forehand. This is not the case, however. In a turn on the forehand the object is primarily to get the horse to move his hindquarters away from his rider's inside leg, placed just behind the girth. The horse should be balanced with equal weight over all four legs, and although the hindquarters move round the forehand, the forefeet should not pivot. This is the only instance when the rider's inside leg may be drawn back, and once the horse has understood the exercise it is of no further use in his training.

To ride a turn on the forehand, position

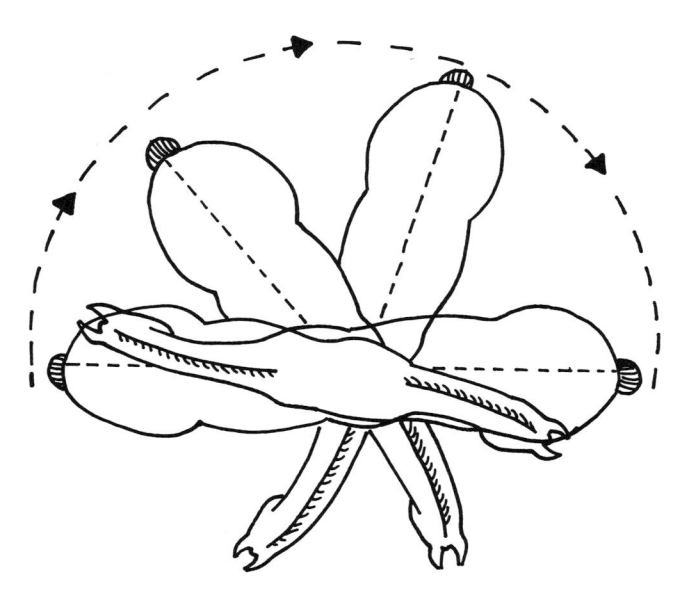

Turn on the forehand.

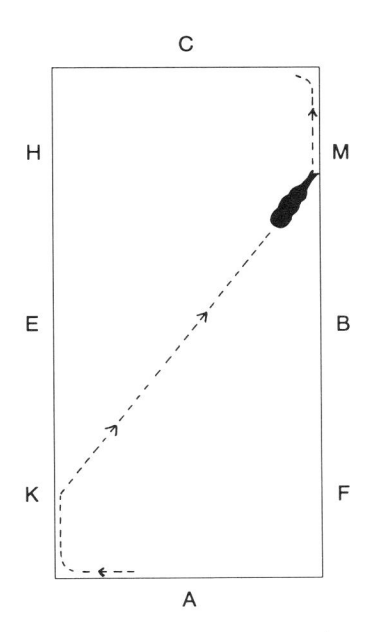

FURTHER SCHOOLING ON THE FLAT

Position of the horse ready for a turn on the forehand.

the horse at the end of a diagonal facing the quarter marker (see diagram). Bring him to a square halt, with his head flexed very slightly to the inside. Then ask him to move his hindquarters into the track. As soon as he is in the track he can be ridden forwards round the school in the normal manner.

Leg-Yield

In a leg-yield the horse should progress forwards and also sideways, with a slight flexion away from the direction in which he is travelling. The purpose is to make him more responsive to the rider's inside leg, and to teach the rider to use that leg effectively.

A good way to teach the horse leg-yield is to position him about 3m in from, and

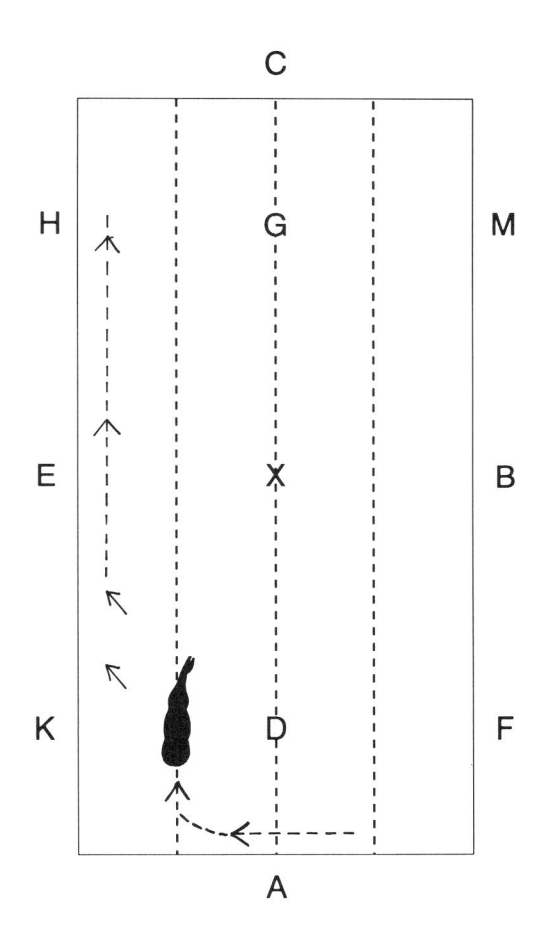

Leg-yielding away from the right leg.

parallel to, the track (see diagram). Once begun, the exercise may be achieved by riding a few steps of leg-yield, followed by riding forwards straight, followed by a few more steps of leg-yield. In this way the horse may be controlled and will not get the chance to fall sideways. A schooling whip can be used behind the rider's inside leg as support, while the outside leg controls the hindquarters and the degree of sideways movement. The reins should be used to keep the horse's forehand

FURTHER SCHOOLING ON THE FLAT

A fault that is often seen: the hindquarters are trailing and the horse is allowed to fall on his shoulder.

A good leg-yield in spite of the rider's left leg being rather far back.

aligned (shoulders, neck and head) so that he is kept as straight as possible, and the rider must aim for, and look at, a predetermined marker.

The exercise may be ridden in walk and trot, and can be used on straight lines and on circles. When ridden on a circle, the curve already adopted by the size of the circle may increase momentarily while the horse makes his response, then the normal curve resumed.

It is also possible to make the horse yield to the leg in canter, but care must be taken not to ask more than a stride or two because the canter pace does not permit the legs to cross each other as they can in walk or trot.

Shoulder-in

Once the horse has learned to yield to the leg, the rider should start to take extra control of the forehand. The shoulder-in exercise provides this opportunity, as well as furthering engagement of the horse's inside leg and promoting suppleness.

The shoulder-in may be introduced to the horse on the long side of the school following preparation on a 10m circle (see diagram). It may be started at walk to give rider and horse a chance to organize themselves. On the circle the rider should make the horse attend to the aids and the bend. On completion of the circle the horse

FURTHER SCHOOLING ON THE FLAT

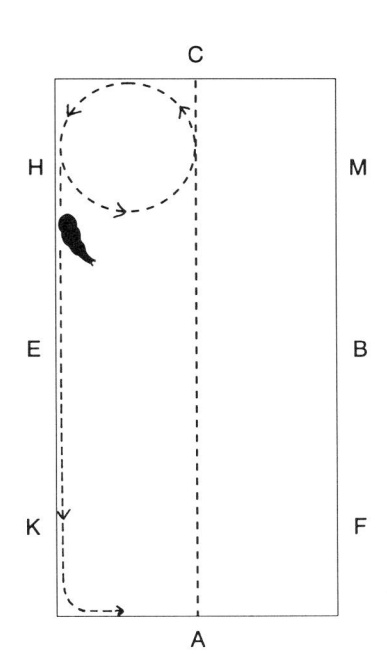

Using a ten-metre circle in preparation for a shoulder-in.

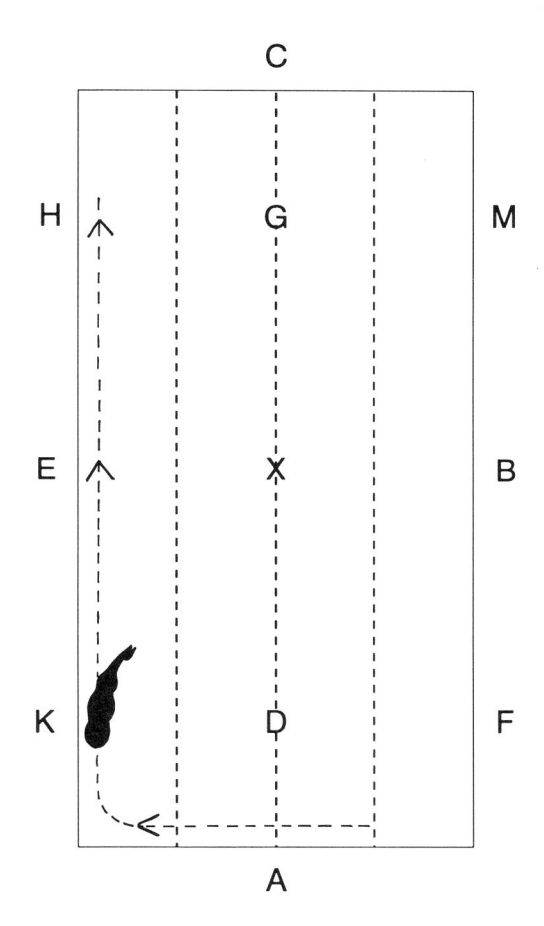

Shoulder-in right.

should be asked to go large, but maintaining the bend of the circle. His forehand should be in the position of no more than a 45 degree angle to the track (see diagram); this may be less when he is starting, but whatever angle is taken, it should be maintained. Only a few steps at a time should be ridden in the early stages, the horse being taken onto a circle again, or he may be made straight and ridden forwards.

The rider's inside leg is responsible for impulsion and bend, while the outside leg encourages bend and controls the hindquarters. He must keep the forehand in position with the reins, that is to say, at the angle he has chosen. The inside rein will maintain a slight flexion away from the direction in which the horse is travelling, while the outside rein supports the horse's shoulder and the degree of forward movement.

A common problem is that the rider uses more inside rein than outside, causing the horse to curl his neck inwards and fall onto his outside shoulder.

A correctly ridden shoulder-in should improve the paces and give the rider greater control.

The exercise known as shoulder-in position or shoulder fore is a lesser degree of the same movement and should be used when preparing the horse for most exer-

FURTHER SCHOOLING ON THE FLAT

The rider is attempting shoulder-in but has pulled the horse's head round, causing him to resist. The neck should not show a greater bend than the rest of the horse.

A better position but should show more bend through the body and less angle.

cises and in helping to straighten him. Its use puts the forehand in a position of balance so that the horse can more easily respond to the aids. In canter it is particularly helpful when the hindquarters come in away from the side of the school or during a circle. If the rider should try to straighten the horse by pushing the hindquarters out, the effect is for the horse merely to move his whole body out, which still leaves the hindquarters curling inwards.

Riders should not underestimate the value of shoulder-in and shoulder-in position, and should incorporate it into all the work that is done.

Collection

In order to achieve a good shoulder-in and to be able to ride the more advanced exercises such as pirouette, rein back and lateral movements as described below, the horse should be collected. Collection is the improved engagement of the horse so that he is able to use himself more effectively. The steps or strides may be shorter and higher, but only as a result of good engagement and impulsion. The rider should obtain collection as follows: first the rider should sit correctly (*see* Chapter 4), then he should increase the influence of his legs to make the horse more active so that he engages his hind legs under his body. At the same time, the rider's hands

FURTHER SCHOOLING ON THE FLAT

Although this rider is actually asking for piaffe steps in order to engage the hindquarters, the picture demonstrates how the horse is gathered together for collection and how the lowered hindquarters physically raise the forehand.

will also increase their influence, asking the horse to arch his neck, flex at the poll and yield to the bit. If all this happens as it should, the horse's frame should adopt a shorter and more 'uphill' outline, whilst still maintaining roundness.

When teaching the horse to collect, only a few steps at a time should be asked and if there is any loss of impulsion the horse should immediately be sent forwards. Most horses resist collection because it is difficult, and they may show this resistance by fighting the bit, stiffening the back or swinging the hindquarters.

Whilst being sympathetic to the horse's problems, the rider should not be put off by such resistance but should quietly persevere, making sure that his aids are correct.

Mistakes that are commonly made in relation to collection are that the rider restricts the paces, and instead of the steps springing more, they become shorter and flatter. Also, instead of the hindquarters being brought under the horse to lift his forehand, the neck is pulled up with the nose pulled in, and no difference in the position of the hindquarters.

In collection the rider should feel that his horse is going forwards eagerly, that his back is soft and yielding to sit on and that he is light and easy to steer

FURTHER SCHOOLING ON THE FLAT

through the relevant movements. He should feel that the shoulders are lifting, not dropping.

Walk Pirouette

This should be performed from a collected walk and should be taught to the horse by degrees, perhaps by first riding it on a square (see Chapter 8). The rider should ask for a couple of steps only to start with, then a 90° turn and finally a 180° turn.

The horse should bring his forehand round his hindquarters, which should describe a very small turn with the inside hind leg stepping on the spot. He should be curved to the inside and be kept in a round outline.

The object of the exercise is to further the engagement of the hindquarters, especially the inside hind leg, and give the rider more control.

If the pirouette is developed from the square, each corner may be utilized to build up to the riding of the 90° turn. The rider should position the horse for the corner, and when he wants to do the turn he proceeds as follows: he must keep his inside leg firmly in place to hold the bend, to prevent the horse from falling round too quickly and to keep up the impulsion. The inside rein holds the flexion while the outside rein controls the collection and forward movement by means of half-halts (see Chapter 6) and also asks the horse to turn. From the feel of the outside rein against his neck the horse should turn, and providing the rider's outside leg holds the quarters, a pirouette may be accomplished.

Most riders fail to keep the bend through the turn, which unbalances the horse. Also their outside leg is not used

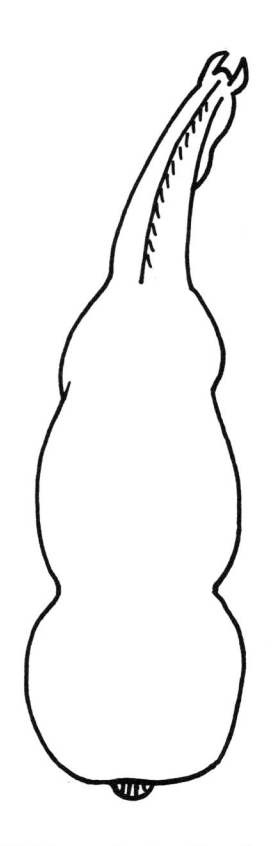

Taking a flexion (head only).

effectively to assist in holding the bend, and fails to prevent the hindquarters from stepping outwards. Too much tension on the inside rein will also hinder the turn, causing the hindquarters to go in the opposite direction to that which is required.

The rider may influence and help his horse by using slight alterations of weight during the turn to assist balance, but he should beware of sitting too strongly on the seatbone away from the direction in which he wants to go as this can make it difficult for the horse and harder to hold the bend.

If the horse is slow to understand, the

FURTHER SCHOOLING ON THE FLAT

rider may benefit from using his whip in his outside hand, but then he must be careful that the horse does not swing round too quickly instead. Also, the horse must be prevented from going forwards or backwards.

Rein-Back

The horse may be required to step backwards for a variety of reasons, so it is useful to be able to do it without fuss. Most horses resist when they are introduced to this movement because they simply do not understand what is wanted.

A square, balanced halt is first required, with the horse on the aids. The rider should then ask the horse to step forwards using gentle leg aids; but as he responds, the rein aids are applied, if necessary alternately, restricting forward movement. The horse may hesitate but then, feeling the reins preventing a forward step, he may take a step back. He should be rewarded immediately and ridden forwards. Only when he has fully grasped the initial step back should further steps be added; and do not expect these to be smooth at first. Each step should be rewarded by an easing of the hands before the next aid is given. Up to six steps is the normal number to aim for. The horse should be kept straight and in a round outline, and he will find the exercise easier if his poll is kept at the highest point with his head in an almost vertical position.

Do not practise the rein-back too early on in the horse's training when the back muscles are weak. Also, always check that the halt is not being spoilt because the horse is anticipating the rein-back movement.

Lateral Work

This includes half-pass, renvers (tail to the wall) and travers (head to the wall). The diagrams show where these movements may best be ridden. These exercises develop the horse physically and encourage suppleness, although many riders find them difficult to ride because of the good co-ordination needed. Also the horse himself often finds them awkward at first.

In all lateral movements the horse should bend towards the direction in which he is travelling. His curve should be uniform through his length, and he should travel forwards towards a designated marker bent round his rider's inside leg. In half-pass the degree of bend is deter-

Travers (head to wall), is a good way to prepare the horse for other lateral work. This shows good bend and angle.

FURTHER SCHOOLING ON THE FLAT

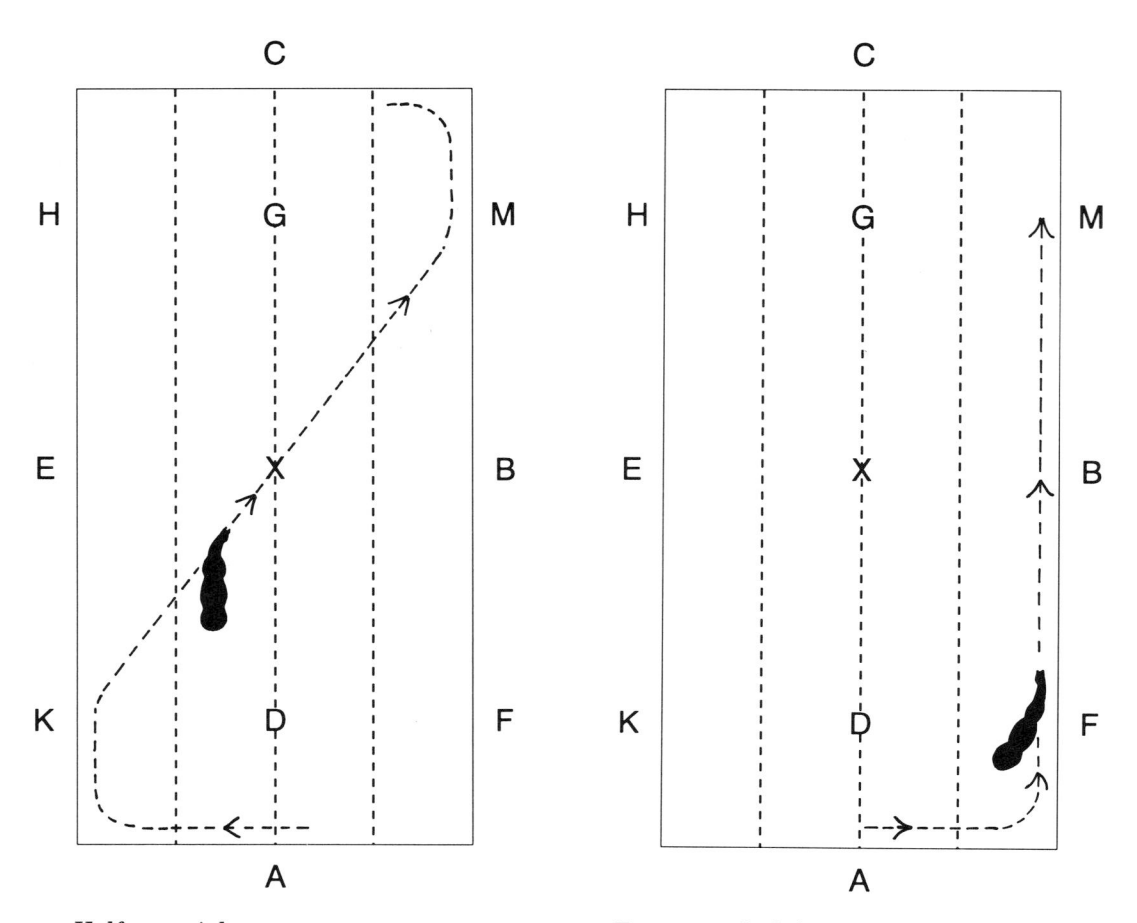

Half-pass right.

Travers to the left.

mined by the angle of the movement, such that the bend is less if travelling from a quarter marker to G in a 60 x 20m arena than if going from a quarter marker to X in a 40 x 20m arena (see diagram).

Many faults occur because the rider fails to position his horse's shoulders towards the marker he is aiming for, ending up in a leg-yield instead. The horse can only keep up his engagement and impulsion if the movement is ridden properly.

The rider should ride energetically with his inside leg to create bend and forward momentum. His outside rein should control the pace and keep the collection. The inside rein should ask for and keep the flexion as it would normally when bending the horse, while the outside leg is responsible for the hindquarters being placed around the rider's inside leg. This leg should not drive the horse sideways, although of course the horse must respond to it.

When this stage of training is reached, lateral work should be fitted into the

FURTHER SCHOOLING ON THE FLAT

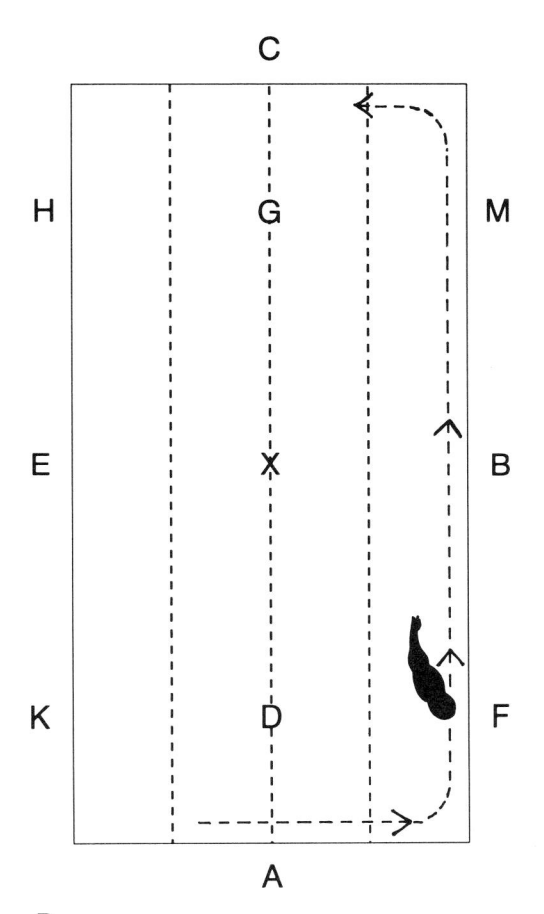

Renvers.

general training and must not be thought of as a separate exercise.

Extension

Once the horse can be collected, he is in a position to extend. He has learned to engage and come together, to remain on the aids, and to do transitions smoothly. He has been taught variations within each pace and can remain in balance, and from these beginnings a gradual enlargement of the pace can be made, which at each stage should be well controlled.

In more advanced dressage and eventing competitions the horse will be required to show medium and extended strides in all paces, the medium having grown from the working paces and the extension being the maximum that each horse can give. All the fundamental principles apply, those of straightness, balance, rhythm, regularity, correct outline and obedience. Transitions into and out of extensions must be clear and smooth, and without resistance.

All extensions are obtained from a build-up of energy which is contained, then used in a regulated fashion. The rider must sit securely, be able to use his legs effectively and allow the horse to stretch his frame. This must not be done in such a way that he comes off the aids, but should be the result of a general release of compressed energy.

It is most important that the horse is brought together again after the extension by being sent forwards into his bridle with the leg, and not simply pulled back with the hand and no support from the seat and legs.

Counter-canter

This is a suppling and balancing exercise where the horse must remain bent to the leading leg. It is generally taught before the flying change.

Flying Change, or Change in the Air

In canter it is very useful when jumping,

FURTHER SCHOOLING ON THE FLAT

and quite fun in any case, to be able to change rein without having to trot and then strike off again on a new lead. Before the flying change can be attempted, however, the horse must know clearly how to strike off into canter correctly when told, without coming off the aids, and this must be equally good on both reins. Thus he must be able to canter in a straight line on one lead, trot, and then strike off into the opposite lead with no hesitation or confusion, and apart from an appropriate bend over the leading leg, remain absolutely straight.

The next step is gradually to reduce the number of trot steps between the transition from one canter to another. He must not resist, become crooked, or anticipate. Eventually, once this work is established, the rider may ask for the change of leg while remaining in canter, but he must be extra clear in giving his aids. At first the horse, being surprised, may fall back to trot, leap forwards or change leg in front or behind only, causing him to be disunited. If this happens he should be brought to trot, made calm and the procedure begun again.

It is important for the rider to keep a good position in the saddle so that he can best help the horse at what can be a difficult moment for him. Swinging the horse to the side is often used as a method of getting him to change legs, but as this causes him to become unbalanced it is unwise to perform a change in this way. Sometimes a schooling whip is needed to make the aids clearer, especially if the horse is inclined to be idle.

A good canter is absolutely essential because the horse can only change in the moment of suspension, and achieving this canter does require good engagement and collection. It should feel active and have plenty of bounce, and this energy should be achieved without creating tension, as any anxiety in the horse brings about problems.

There are several common difficulties connected to teaching changes. First of all, it is not particularly easy to give a strong enough aid without making the horse either put his head in the air, or try to dash off. In either case it is a waste of time trying to follow through as the horse is not in a position to obey. He must be taught to remain round and stay in control.

The next problem may be that the horse will change but only in front or behind, thus causing the canter to become disunited. Sometimes if the rider reinforces his leg aid with the whip, the pace may be made true, but more often than not the horse has to be brought back to trot and the exercise begun again.

Usually the rider or horse will find it easier to change in one direction than in the other, a circumstance which is related to the horse's favourite lead or to the rider's stronger side. If this is the case, then concentration on the easy side will ensure that both horse and rider get the feel of what is wanted before tackling the exercise on the other rein.

Certain exercises can be used before asking for a change, which help in its successful performance. These include riding 10m circles, which help to set up the right sort of canter and get the horse supple and attentive to the aids. Then you could ride a 10m half circle returning to the track at the half or quarter marker, asking for a change as you regain the outside track.

There are also several other places in the school that also encourage the flying change:

- At the end of a diagonal just before reaching the track.
- Crossing the school from the half markers; a change can be asked for at X, or before the turn on the opposite side.
- After a canter half-pass as the track is reached.
- From one 20m circle as you change to another on a figure-of-eight.
- From 10m half circles you regain the outside track.
- From counter-canter.

Feeling whether a change is true can only come from practice; but as far as the horse is concerned, he can only do what is wanted if the rider coordinates the aids with a change of bend that allows the legs to follow through correctly. Any resistance in his mouth, or stiffness in his body, will result in late changes, swinging of the hindquarters or other problems.

When the horse has been taught changes he may then anticipate them and for a time will make mistakes, offering them when not required. Do not be impatient if this happens, however. Stay calm and make the aids clearer to the horse, and he will soon learn to differentiate.

The aim in all training is to advance the horse's mental and physical capacity so that he can do what he is asked. He will also become more pleasant to ride and a willing companion. However, this state can only be achieved progressively, by building brick by brick, and by consolidating through practice each stage of training so that the structure is made strong. Whenever there is anxiety on the part of either horse or rider, return to something easier.

Watching

It is well worthwhile attending a dressage competition purely to watch these movements ridden, but it may be necessary to find a show where riders of international calibre take part to see them ridden as they should be.

Developing Feel

Developing feel for these movements will take some time, and it cannot be rushed. The horse himself is a good critic as he will make it plain when he cannot do something, either by resisting in his mouth or by losing impulsion. Although it is important not to give in to such resistance, if he continues to object it is a good idea to check thoroughly what you are asking and how.

CHAPTER 10
Hacking Out

Roadwork

For some people, riding on the roads may be entirely impractical, especially if they live in a built-up area or beside a motorway. It is not even essential to do so, although it can have several useful advantages. Before even contemplating taking a horse on the roads, however, some preparation may be done at home: first, the horse might be introduced to the sight of a vehicle and the sound of a running engine. Some vehicles are very smelly, too, and even this can be frightening for the horse. He should then, if possible, be taken to a safe place where he can become used to the noise and speed of traffic without actually being on a road. Another horse already accustomed to it should go with him to give him confidence, and he should be constantly reassured by his rider.

Inevitably, for one reason or another, some horses become nervous in traffic. They may just be frightened of large noisy lorries, or it could be speeding motor bikes or rushing cars, and some can even be silly about cyclists! Fear of traffic is understandable – I am often frightened of it myself! – but however sympathetic one feels, a frightened horse is potentially dangerous and such animals are best kept off the roads for everybody's safety. Naughtiness is another matter, being a form of napping; this should be dealt with quickly, and should not be allowed to develop. Determining whether the horse's reaction is because of fear or due to naughtiness is not always simple, but if you really know your horse I am sure you will be able to decide.

Equipment for the Horse

Before any horse is taken on the roads he should be properly shod, and he may need road studs; your farrier can advise on this subject. Some people like to ride out in exercise knee pads, just in case the horse should stumble or slip. I know from past experience how traumatic it can be to have a horse come down on the road, and how long broken knees can take to heal; so I would recommend riders to use them.

Always ride out in a bridle to which the horse is accustomed and which gives sufficient control, and make sure that the leatherwork is sound. Broken reins at any time are a disaster, but on the roads they could be fatal. Of course, the saddle should fit the horse in any case, but if it is likely to be on his back for some considerable time, extra care must be taken to see that it is not likely to rub or to cause sores. Using a saddle cloth or a sheepskin may help to save his back.

In winter when it is very cold a three-quarter blanket under the saddle may help to keep the horse warm; similarly a rain sheet will keep him dry over his loins.

HACKING OUT

When on the roads it is wise to put boots on the horse and/or exercise knee pads to save him from possible injury.

Bandaging the legs for exercise should not be done as a general practice, as it can restrict the tendons and affect circulation. If bandages are used for a particular reason they should be put over some suitable material (padding supplied by a saddler) and, most important, care taken that the tension is distributed evenly.

Boots of varying types may be used for extra protection.

Road Code for the Rider

The first most important thing to know when riding out is the Highway Code. Even if you are not a driver, I believe this is essential as it tells the rider what to expect from those who do drive; and there are specific rules for the rider to follow when, for example, turning right or left at traffic lights, crossing at junctions and roundabouts, and passing stationary vehicles. Study the road safety literature supplied by the British Horse Society, too: this will not only tell you how to ride on the roads and how to behave, it can also provide advice on insurance and legal matters, how to cope in an emergency, and it gives information about protective and high-visibility clothing for horse and rider.

The main criterion is to use your common sense, and not to put yourself, the horse or others into a situation where they

HACKING OUT

are at risk. Holding up traffic unnecessarily is selfish; and failing to thank drivers if they slow down is bad manners, and does not encourage them to do so next time. Also, if it is safe to wave a driver past you, then do so – he will undoubtedly be grateful.

Unfortunately it is a sad fact that many drivers nowadays are unsympathetic to animals on the roads, and some even delight in frightening them. It is important to be aware of this, and therefore always to keep your wits about you, and to anticipate trouble; in this way you may be able to prevent accidents. Always take a whip: you may need it to help you get the horse past something that he doesn't like.

Hacking for Pleasure

Riding out can be pleasurable, but it will not be unless horse and rider are fit enough for the length of time they wish to go out. Also, the rider must be capable, and novices should only venture out under strict supervision from an experienced person.

Consider Your Horse

Hacking is not an excuse to ride badly – the rider may enjoy himself, but his horse will not. It is remarkable, too, how many riders appear to lack any sympathy towards their horses; they can often be seen hammering along at a fast trot, causing unnecessary jarring to their back and legs. Nor is the horse's mouth there to be used as a lever to help the rider rise to the trot! The way a rider sits in the saddle is also an indication of his sensitivity – or lack of it. Thumping the body back down into the saddle, especially near the horse's loins, is very bad for him and can cause considerable damage, quite apart from being very tiring.

It is my opinion that there are far too many horses to be seen nowadays in poor condition, trailing along in a dispirited fashion and evidently in considerable suffering. I am sure that riders do not deliberately inflict cruelty on their horses, but they really should realize that a horse with all his ribs showing, or one that is grossly fat, cannot be happy.

Planning Your Hack

Plan how far to go and decide what speed or pace to ride at. Much of the time may be spent in walk admiring the countryside, but be aware while doing this that there are hazards, and that the horse may shy, so do not have the reins so long that they cannot be of immediate use in a crisis.

Ensure that you can open and shut a gate while you are mounted. It isn't difficult to teach your horse this manoeuvre, although it sometimes requires a little patience as the horse may back away, leaving you stranded halfway between himself and the gate! The sensible approach is to stand next to the gate to undo the latch, then to push it open and walk through, holding on to it so it doesn't blow back and hit you or the horse on the way. Then push it shut and stand next to it again to latch it. Some gates need lifting, which can be awkward, but I have seldom found a horse which would not stand if taught to do so. Of course, the training that you do in the school will help because if the horse understands the meaning of the aids, and has learned to be obedient and wishes to please, then he will almost certainly cooperate.

HACKING OUT

When opening gates, leave plenty of room for the horse to pass through. It is tiresome to have to dismount, so the horse should be taught to stand while they are opened and shut.

Decide on a comfortable length of stirrup before you start – and never set out on a hack without them. Very short stirrups can be tiring and put the weight too near the horse's loins; long ones can cause the seat to be insecure. Besides, being comfortable is essential to enjoyment!

Hacking for Fitness

What is achieved on a hack depends on its purpose. If it is entirely for pleasure the rider may take out his horse every day, but there could be several other reasons for hacking. It may be to introduce a young horse to roadwork, and the object is for him to gain experience of new sights and sounds; or it may be to give an older horse a break from normal routine; or fitness may be the objective.

Planning a Fitness Routine

If the objective is to achieve fitness, a careful routine should be planned. To begin with the horse should be given slow work over a short distance, then build this up to longer periods of trotting. Constant attention must be paid to the horse's feet and soundness when doing this sort of work.

When roadwork is used as an aid to fitness, the gradually increasing distance must be combined with extra food. The horse's intake of bulk forage feed – hay or grass – may need to be cut down and his 'short' – concentrate – feed increased, perhaps with supplements added. The relationship of work to feed must be under constant review.

Getting the horse fit will involve mainly walk and trot work with faster work once or twice a week, as well as normal schooling. The horse must also learn to go up- and downhill, and to canter safely over difficult terrain. The fitness required will depend on whether the horse is to go round a local hunter trial or a BHS event, but whatever it is, he should be able to do the job he is asked to do without showing signs of distress. The amount he sweats, his breathing and his pulse (the normal rate is 36–42 beats to the minute) should indicate to his rider his state of fitness.

Keeping to a routine will not only help the horse but also the rider, and as each horse will vary in his ability to become, and remain, fit, every rider should determine a suitable programme for himself as well.

HACKING OUT

Once the horse is fit, he will need a good deal of exercise and must not be left shut in his stable for the day. He may be turned out or lunged if the rider is short of time, but otherwise should be exercised properly. A fit horse is tiring to ride and the rider should expect his own stamina to match his horse.

If the intention is to get the horse ready for a particular competition the build-up of exercise and fitness will continue until that event. Once it is over, the rider must remember that his horse will probably find it hard to simply 'switch off', and he cannot be just chucked out into a field without physical hardship: he should be let down just as gradually by a slow and carefully devised reduction of work and food.

Cooling the Horse Down

It is important that the horse is properly cooled off at the end of a hack. If he is already fit he may not get very hot at all, but may only do so as he is becoming fit. Nevertheless, he should always be walked for some distance at the end of a hack so that he is brought back cool; alternatively if he is still very warm he may be washed off and then dried and rugged up; or he may be dried off by rubbing him down with hay or straw.

He should *never* be left to get cold, and if he tends to break out, a longer period of cooling may be necessary.

Young Horses

Young horses should always be taken out with an older horse to start with, and if possible they should be ridden abreast with the younger one on the inside. When passing vehicles head on, the older horse can give a lead; also if there are roadworks or other potentially alarming objects.

Hacking out gives all horses the chance to go forwards, a quality which is so important in their training. There is also the interest factor, since the route is bound to provide variety, from which both horse and rider may benefit.

Several riders may wish to hack together, and this can be good experience generally – and it should also teach all concerned about control! Remember, however, that galloping about in a group can be extremely dangerous, and although grass verges or the edge of the farmer's field will be tempting, do be aware that horses may readily become over-excited. Remember, too, that horses like to be together, and one on its own, or which becomes separated can be quite nappy and difficult, and even potentially dangerous.

Hacking for Schooling

There are various reasons why a rider may wish to school his horse while out on the roads: his arena may be having attention, the paddock may be too wet or muddy, or he is simply combining a fitness programme with schoolwork. It always surprises me when people say they haven't been able to school their horse for a week because they have only been able to hack out; I find that so much can be achieved on a hack!

Many roads are no pleasure to ride on today, however, because of traffic, and because of the often rather unpleasant adverse camber which seems to draw you into the side. I have been fortunate and have lived in places where there were grass verges, even if intermittent,

HACKING OUT

or headlands, the occasional hay- or cornfield, or woodland places where it was nearly always possible to find a path to school on. And in my jumping days it seemed there was always a drainage ditch or a fallen tree to pop a youngster over, or later on when we were more ambitious, inviting hedges or rails that could be jumped at little risk either to myself or to the owner's property.

The Country Code

Consideration for other people's land should be a high priority when out hacking. Being able to ride away from the roads is obviously more pleasurable, quite apart from being better for the horse's legs, but some landowners will not permit horse riding due to past abuse and it is clearly very important not to offend those who are still prepared to allow it. All land is precious and, as horse owners, we should appreciate that if we are permitted to go on it we should abide by certain rules.

It may seem impossible to resist a good gallop across a tempting green field – but that field may be valuable pasture for grazing, or a cultivated ley for hay or silage; even a cut cornfield may be undersown with some other crop. To canter through corn or hay is plainly thoroughly inconsiderate and stupid; similarly it would be equally foolish to charge through an apple orchard, knocking the fruit to the ground! *Never* leave gates open, thus enabling stock to stray: this is a mortal sin. It is also a criminal offence to allow your dog to worry sheep or cattle; this is particularly distressing to the farmer if they are in lamb or near to calving.

When the weather is wet it is even more important to ride with care and consideration, as woodland rides and paths may become cut up and muddy. Go more slowly, even only at walk, when it is very wet.

Although all these points may seem obvious on the written page, I wonder how many of you *do* discipline yourselves to keep to headlands, to stay off the land when it is wet, and diligently to close and latch all gates?

Schooling on the Road

If nothing else is available the road can provide a good opportunity to practise riding straight – aim at something further ahead – or to develop a good rhythm – the footfalls are easily heard. The ear can become so well attuned that it can soon pick up the sound of a horse that is not level or one that has lost a shoe.

The roads are also an ideal place to practise transitions – I even used to canter sometimes for a short distance – using a patch of nettles or a dock or some such natural feature for markers. Halts, leg-yields and other lateral work can be worked on providing there is no traffic at the time.

Bend can be adopted with the curve of a lane, and collection developed. Some differences of pace can be achieved, although I would never do extensions on the road; however, a large field is ideal for this purpose! I also taught my pony flying changes in a friendly farmer's field; and a very lazy horse which normally would not extend its trot became quite animated up a long grassy valley!

Coming home, when the horse naturally perks up because he is thinking about his stable or his friends, is an ideal place to practise engaging the hind-

HACKING OUT

quarters; or if you feel more ambitious, you might teach the horse to piaffe and passage – but that is another story!

Some horses do not like going away from home and may resort to napping, and this can be serious if the animal refuses to go out of the yard. A very firm line must be taken at the outset, because if the horse wins this battle, the rider is for ever at his mercy.

When combining hacking and schooling the rider should choose the exercises he wishes to work on, and whereabouts on the hack he intends to perform them. When not working on an exercise the horse should be allowed to relax, although the rider must always be in control for safety's sake. Many riders ask me whether the horse should be on the bit when on a hack; my answer is that, when ridden, a horse should always be on the bit, to a lesser or greater degree!

CHAPTER 11
Gymnastic Jumping

The most important thing to remember when jumping is introduced into the horse's training, is to relate the flatwork which he should already know to the work over fences. If the horse is bold and his flatwork has been done properly he should have no difficulty in coping with fences, as long as they are not too high at first. Presentation at a fence and recovery after jumping it will be simple provided he goes straight, remains balanced and allows his rider to keep him on the aids.

The rider must of course be able to keep a secure position so that he does not interfere with his horse, and he should be supple enough to stay with him in moments of crisis. A good saddle that promotes a correct position is naturally a big advantage.

As far as bitting is concerned, each horse's attitude is so different that it is difficult to offer guidance. A big, strong animal may need something more effective in his mouth than one that is weaker

If the training has been correct, bigger fences can be negotiated without difficulty. The rider has presented the horse properly to the fence and is allowing freedom for him to jump.

GYMNASTIC JUMPING

or lazier. Whatever is chosen, it must be fitted properly – and a large bit can be just as damaging to the horse's mouth as one that is too small. Also, the rider is responsible for using the bit so that the horse does not suffer.

After a jumping session the rider may find that his horse's mouth is rather less sensitive than normal, but this should be expected as the impulsion needed for jumping may make him stronger ride. The mouth may be softened again during normal school work so that it does not become dull.

As with flatwork, it is important that the horse is schooled on suitable going. When he is learning this may best be done in the school.

Work over Poles

Schooling the horse over poles is of enormous benefit as a starting point because it promotes his activity, cadence, outline, obedience and flexibility, and it also teaches the rider to follow the movement. Poles may be placed on a straight line, on a circle or a diagonal, anywhere in fact where they may be incorporated into the normal riding of simple school exercises. The horse should be expected to walk or trot, but not canter, calmly over them. As he does so he should be allowed to find his own way, looking to see where he is going, stretching his head and neck out and downwards. The rider should sit close, inclining his body

Poles should be correctly spaced for trotting for each individual horse. The outline in this picture is rather hollow. The horse should be working in a round shape as you would expect for flat work.

GYMNASTIC JUMPING

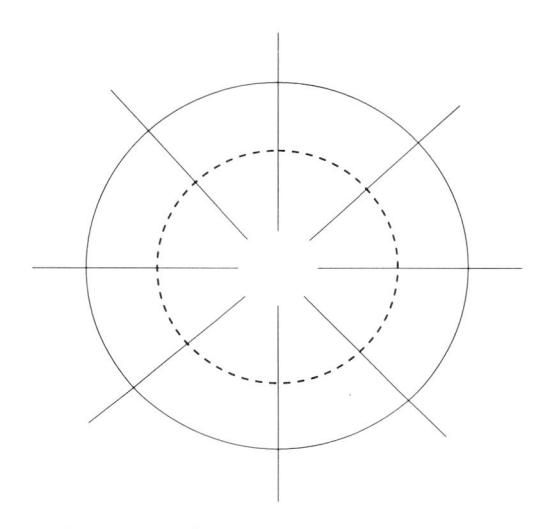

Poles on a circle.

forwards but not tipping up, and should maintain a light, but not an interfering contact.

In between the pole or poles the rider should check the horse's balance and make sure that he is accepting the aids as he should. If he attempts to rush or get his head up he should be quietly restrained and made more obedient to the aids. If he is idle or does not pick up his feet, he should be encouraged to be more active with the schooling whip.

Polework can also be used to teach the horse to keep a bend to the same direction, or to learn to change his bend while actually going over a pole. The rider should use poles to practise his approaches, sometimes riding for the centre, sometimes to one side or the other; in this way the horse will learn to pay attention to his rider, and not simply dash at the poles in a haphazard way.

Rustic poles, plain poles or ones with stripes or blobs of coloured paint should be progressively introduced so that the horse learns to cope with new and unexpected sights. The distances between them should also be varied to keep the horse alert. As a basis, poles are usually set for trotting approximately 4ft (1.2m) apart, and up to about six in a line may be used. Alternate poles may be withdrawn in order to vary the distances, but the rhythm and control should remain the same. The rider should use his own ingenuity to make the work interesting and varied, whilst retaining essential principles.

The Horse's Attitude

It is useful to observe the various attitudes that horses adopt during this work. Some of them are plainly horrified at the sight of even one pole, let alone several, and this sort needs a good deal of patience and persuasion to accept each new pole added. This should be done calmly in walk at first, so that if the horse steps on one of the poles he does not frighten himself. Horses are so often put off because poles have moved about and trip them up, which frightens them rather than teaching them to go over them.

Animals which are nervous or hesitant may be indicating through this attitude that jumping is not their metier. Bold horses, on the other hand, often refuse to walk or trot, and the very sight of a pole incites them to gallop. However, to allow them to do this would be a great mistake from the point of view of controlling them, so they must be persuaded to go calmly. This can take even more patience as the exercise may have to be repeated many times. Circling is a good way to prevent a horse rushing, and may be done at any time during an approach until he is calm.

GYMNASTIC JUMPING

It is interesting, I think, to observe how the horse looks at the poles, whether he eyes them up, adjusting his stride if necessary to avoid touching them; and how he reacts if he does touch them: is there an instant look of panic, or does he still appear calm? Calmness, and not to have liked hitting a pole is ideal, as will be apparent the next time the horse goes over them.

The Horse's Technique

Although the degree to which the horse rounds his back (bascule) will be more obvious when he jumps a proper fence, the way he lowers his head and looks at the poles, and the way his back can lift and swing as he goes over them, is a fair indication of what his natural jumping style will be.

Most of the benefit of polework comes from trotting the horse over them. In the approach he should be well on the aids with his head a little lower than for ordinary schoolwork: this discourages him from getting his head too high, it teaches him to remain round, and is easier for control. His steps should feel active, taking him forwards energetically, and as he sizes up the pole or poles he may raise his head a little and go more firmly into the bridle. As he does so, providing he is keeping his balance and rhythm and is not pulling, the rider should go with him, maintaining contact with the legs and hands.

If the horse is going freely forwards on his own initiative, the rider's legs will only need to sustain the impulsion, and the hands to allow the horse to stretch his head and neck. If on the other hand the horse hesitates, the rider's legs should close instantly to urge him forwards while still maintaining contact with his mouth. A whip should be carried to reinforce the leg aid if necessary.

Rider Technique

As the horse travels over the poles the rider should maintain the contact with legs and hands with his body inclined forwards slightly; the body should absorb the movement of the horse and not stiffen against it. The pace will feel extra springy and can be unseating, but it is important to stay as close to the horse as possible.

Once the poles are negotiated the horse may need restraining if impulsion has increased, or he may need driving on if it has died away. If the horse feels as if he is wandering off a straight line he should instantly be corrected, as he should if he has come off the aids. It is important not to interfere with the horse's natural ability while still retaining control.

Cavaletti

Once the horse and rider can negotiate poles efficiently, a small fence should be introduced, and a cavaletto is ideal for this purpose. It may initially be introduced at the end of a line of trotting poles so that the horse meets it when he is already doing what is familiar to him. It should then not present any problem.

When the cavaletto has been fully accepted, the final pole of the row should be removed and the cavaletto raised to a higher position. Arriving at it, the horse will be expected to make his first real jump. On landing, any loss of balance or control should be regained immediately.

It is the rider's responsibility to determine the line to follow as he approaches

GYMNASTIC JUMPING

the cavaletto: he may wish to go straight ahead, or he may prefer to circle after a couple of strides, but his intentions should be clear to the horse and not left until the last minute.

Once work has been established in this way and if the horse is calm and obedient, cross-poles may then replace the cavaletto, or any other small fence of the rider's choosing. Gradually the poles leading to the fence can be removed, although the fifth pole may be left until last as it is a useful placing pole.

Many trainers use a line of cavaletti on the lowest rung to improve their horse's rhythm in trot and to give pupils more of a feeling of motion. Riders can use them for their own particular purposes, and any such work should be beneficial.

Rider Position and Ability

Pole- and cavaletti work as a preliminary to actual jumping is invaluable to the confidence of both horse and rider. It can be quite fun, it helps the rider to make judgements regarding stride, and it also gives him the chance to strengthen his position. This differs from the flatwork schooling position chiefly in the length of stirrup which will necessarily be shorter for jumping, every joint being flexed to a greater degree. The upper body may incline more forwards but the spine must not collapse. Contact with the legs and hands should be maintained in the same way as for normal schooling.

Before attempting to jump from canter the rider must be thoroughly secure in his position and the horse must have that pace well established. Good balance is crucial, as is willing acceptance of the aids. The horse should be able to maintain a steady speed, and should be able to extend and collect the canter stride.

In addition to normal control the rider must now learn to judge distance, and he must be able to adjust the horse's stride. He may develop this ability by learning to bring his horse's forefeet level with some object on the ground such as a marker placed for this purpose.

He must also learn how to keep the horse round and bent over a fence so that it can land and turn easily, and he should also be able to alter the bend in order to change direction.

It is a great advantage if the horse has been taught to do changes of leg in the air, as better momentum may be kept.

The Jumping Canter

It is important to be able to see, as well as to feel, what a good jumping canter should be like. It should be collected, with the horse gathered together in a well rounded outline. The head may be positioned rather lower than for flatwork, but the principles of putting the horse on the aids are the same. The strides should show plenty of bounce with a well defined period of suspension; this is the moment when all the legs are off the ground at the same time, and it will be at this stage in the stride that the horse takes a fence.

The horse should show a willingness to be controlled, combined with an eagerness to go forwards.

In the approach the horse will first lower his head and neck to assess the fence; he will then arch his back and lower his hindquarters, the hind legs being well underneath the body ready to thrust him into the air. It is important to have watched this process in order to appreciate what you must allow or encourage him to do.

After the fence the horse may temporarily lose balance. This will need to be regained as quickly as possible however, so that if there is another fence it can be approached properly.

Feeling the Canter

In my experience the collected canter feels rather like an arc with the back nicely rounded but in no way tense or rigid. Although the neck may be rather lower than for school work with the nose even behind the vertical, the horse should not feel on his forehand. You should be aware of the hindquarters being well under the body, giving the strides lift. The whole sensation should be one of bounce and spring.

When the pace is lengthened the horse should feel as though he is ready to jump, giving purposeful bounding strides. He should never feel that he has taken control, although he should take the rider to the fence, and not hang back.

A good horse will jump whether he meets the fence correctly or not, and will very often get over it in spite of his rider. He may twist his body to do this or he may arch his back more, hollow, or jump late or early. Whatever he does the rider should be in touch, so close contact is required which even if momentarily lost, can be regained quickly. If this happens it is important to pick up the correct canter again as soon as possible. Everyone becomes unseated at some time or another, but if the horse has been well trained he will automatically expect to resume what he was doing before an upset, so recovery should not take too long.

It is important to be able to sustain momentum over a series of fences, and therefore the aim should be to make the canter so comfortable, obedient and easy to balance that it could be kept up all day.

Combination Fences

The Solid Grid

A solid, purpose-built bounce grid is a good way to improve the horse's agility. Cavaletti can be used for this purpose, but they can be insecure and I prefer a solid grid. Each fence should be about 50cm (1ft 7in) high, with a distance in between of approximately 3.50m (11ft 6in) when ridden in a straight line. The lane has to be purpose-made and should be built of indestructible timber such as telegraph poles. The horse must keep momentum in order to land and take off again immediately. This work develops the horse's athleticism, and the rider must be extremely flexible in order to stay with him.

Combinations

Doubles and trebles or any combination of fences will help to develop the horse's strength and agility and teach him to look at what he is doing and listen to his rider. The approximate distance between two fences with one canter stride between them is 7.3m (24ft) for an average-sized horse and rather less for a pony.

The chief point to bear in mind is to keep fences to a sensible height so as not to overface the horse which may upset his confidence. When horses refuse fences or run out there are several possible reasons why they do so:

GYMNASTIC JUMPING

- The standard of flatwork schooling is unsatisfactory and therefore the rider does not have sufficient control.
- The horse was not prepared properly and was taken by surprise.
- The rider failed to ride with determination.
- The fence was new to the horse, or higher than he had been asked to jump before.
- The horse did not have the capacity to jump the fence and was looking after himself.

There may be other reasons, too, but whatever the problems, always go back to the beginning; this may seem tiresome, but it is worth it in the end.

Loose Jumping

Horses are very clever and can, if agility and training permit, get themselves out of all sorts of difficulties. It is interesting to see how they cope with the different fences presented to them, and how some of the scopey ones will jump themselves out of an awkward or new (to them) situation; those with less ability may get into trouble because they simply have not got the spring. It is essential to assess a horse's capacity and attitude in order to know how best to ride it, and loose jumping is invaluable for this purpose: not only does it give you a chance to weigh up the horse's ability and confidence, but the horse can learn to adjust himself to the different fences he meets without the encumbrance of a rider on his back.

The Feel of Jumping Combinations

Providing the canter is well prepared and the horse has been taught to jump individual obstacles first, jumping combination fences should not be a problem. At home the striding should be worked out for the particular horse, and the distance set so that he learns to take one or two canter strides between fences. At shows the distances between the fences in a combination are sometimes short, sometimes long, but if the horse is supple and on the aids, the rider will be able to make any alterations needed.

The feel is one of continuity, with impulsion being maintained and if necessary increased so that there is energy left for the final part of a line of fences. The horse has to make a tremendous effort to reach and stretch over a spread fence, and the rider must make the same effort to give him the freedom to do this. To jump a high fence the horse must really spring off his hocks, and it is not always easy to stay close while still allowing him freedom of the head and neck. The landing can be especially difficult as it is easy to get left in the air; the rider should aim to recover quickly, gathering up the reins and picking up the contact as soon as he can.

Cross-Country Riding

The rider intending to gallop and jump across country must be certain that he is confident and secure enough in his seat to be able to help the horse and not leave everything to him! Being able to control the pace is very important, first so the horse may be taken steadily into awkward or downhill fences, and second, so the

GYMNASTIC JUMPING

rider can regulate the speed so the horse does not exhaust himself in the first few minutes. Being able to push him on, or to steady him over difficult terrain is essential, as is being able to adjust his pace in relation to the going.

When training the horse for cross-country work his confidence may be helped a great deal if he can follow a companion; this also helps the rider and may prevent problems arising.

As with all jumping work, fences should be small to begin with, and the horse should only be asked to jump bigger or more difficult ones when he is physically strong enough and has been mentally prepared.

Every rider should keep a strict check on his horse's feet and limbs to make sure that he is sound enough for jumping work, and that he is well shod. The use of studs is recommended if you are doing a lot of jumping; the farrier is perhaps the best person to advise on this subject as each horse's feet vary so much.

Watching the Experts

Watch the experts riding across country to see how they present their horse at the different obstacles they meet. It is essential to know at what speed to ride any particular fence; also how to make recoveries and help the horse. To ride well across country requires courage and a positive attitude, both of which may be seen if you observe well known event riders. It is an eye-opener to see how quickly such riders slip the reins deliberately, or when *in extremis* if the horse makes a mistake; and so, too, is the way they can stick on even against all the odds!

It is important to appreciate how fit the horses are, and how they can keep going at a strong gallop and take their fences whilst remaining balanced and controlled. Moreover only those which are supple and obedient can successfully endure the rigours of some of the testing courses they are asked to jump.

What it Feels Like

To ride across country at speed and jump fences can be exhilarating. Horses that look after their riders and get themselves out of a tricky situation are worth their weight in gold; they add considerably to the thrill, too, because they are a real partner in the whole experience – in fact they may take charge of less positive riders!

A horse which pulls is not fun to ride, and can even be a danger; equally it is not a pleasant experience to ride across country unless the horse is really going strongly into his bridle. This is especially true if a rider is somewhat tentative; in this case the bold horse which is going anyway is even more necessary, so as to make up his rider's mind for him! The aim, however, is a partnership in which one helps the other, with full knowledge of each other's capabilities. The horse must be strong and supple, and so must his rider if they are to operate together in close harmony.

A Daily Routine for Jump Training

Loosening Up

First of all you should try to follow a regular pattern for loosening up yourself and your horse: so, walk the horse into

GYMNASTIC JUMPING

your jumping area on a long, but not a loose rein, and aim to walk in a relaxed manner for a few minutes. Of course if the horse is fresh you may have to trot immediately, but it would be better not to do this. As you walk round, try to encourage the horse to take a long stride and to stretch his neck. Make sure he is listening to your leg aids and is going forwards. Keep a contact with his mouth. During this period the horse can see the fences he may be asked to go over later, and has time to become accustomed to their position in the arena, or their colour, or any other factor that might be new to him.

Rider Position for Jumping

As you walk round, check that your stirrups are a suitable length and that your position is as correct as possible. There are no rules about length of stirrups, it is mostly personal preference, but bear in mind that if they are very short it can be difficult to stay in the saddle in moments of crisis, and if they are too long the thighs cannot give sufficient support to the body when it is inclined forwards.

At the loosening up stage you should sit upright, but as soon as the horse takes up a faster pace you should adopt the jumping position. This differs from the flatwork position only in the upper body, because although the stirrups are shortened, it is the angles of the hips, knees and ankles that are altered, not the position of them on the horse. Of course the leg aids are used in a slightly different area but although this is higher up than for flatwork, horses are clever creatures and soon learn to adapt. There are one or two points to guard against, however. One is that the more acute angle of the knee joint does not induce the lower leg to creep back up the horse's flank; this would lead to insecurity of the seat and less effective aids. Also be firm with yourself about the upper body, because if this inclines forwards in the wrong way it will also lead to insecurity. It is important when bringing the body forwards to follow the horse's movement, and to keep your back straight and not allow it to collapse at the waist. If this happens the influence of the seat is instantly lost.

Another point to remember is that the seat should still be in the saddle. Do not stand on your stirrups. Try to take the weight of the body on the thighs and knees, sitting as deeply into the saddle as you can. The seat can then be used to drive the horse forwards when needed, and in that position also allows for the legs to be used effectively.

Now a few words about the hands. When riding on the flat the hands are normally held in the region just above the withers. As you will almost certainly want a shorter rein for jumping the hands will then be further forwards. This does not mean that they should rest on the horse's neck: preferably they should be on either side of it, keeping the same elastic contact as for flatwork. Only in this way can the messages be passed to the horse satisfactorily and control be maintained.

Warming up

When you have finished the period of loosening up, you should then gather the horse together ready for greater action; this should be done just as you would on the flat if you were collecting him. One point I would like to make here is that so often collection is misconstrued and the steps are over-shortened. In some instances this is necessary, but on the whole it is the greater engagement of the horse that is meant, not an alteration of the steps or strides. At any rate emphasis should be put on good activity and impulsion, because without this you will never be able to leave the ground!

It is also very important to keep the horse in a round outline, even a little deep, as this is the best shape for him to be in to operate successfully. You will probably find that as he approaches his fences he will raise his head to look where he is going and to size up the obstacle. Obviously he needs to do this, but if he is already hollow instead of round he will end up above the bit and out of control.

After some trot work around your fences which should get the horse further loosened and bending to each direction, you can begin some canter work. Now you may wish to increase the angle of your body slightly so that you can go with the horse, although the seat should remain in contact with the saddle.

You will need to develop a good jumping canter: this should be very balanced and have plenty of spring, and the horse should be sufficiently collected that he is able to lengthen or shorten his stride at a moment's notice. This is vital to success so should be practised diligently.

Transitions

Any change of pace or alteration of the stride within a pace should be ridden as it would be on the flat, that is to say, smoothly and submissively. A sharp aid can upset the general equilibrium, and any resistance by the horse may change the flow of his stride. When jumping a course the flow or momentum is crucial, and only those riders who are in complete control can really expect good results. The half-halt which is ridden to provide a correction to balance, or to collect the stride, is particularly influential. With novice horses or riders, changes of direction must be achieved through a few trot strides and it is essential to the horse's balance that these are done with care. They should be ridden with the correct bend, and allowing enough time for the horse to adjust from one pace to another.

As he progresses, the horse will learn to remain in canter throughout a course. To do this he must be able to change legs in the air, which should be taught as described in an earlier chapter. It is relatively easy to swing the horse over to get him to change legs but this causes loss of balance and often results in him becoming disunited. Once the horse has been taught how to perform changes it is far easier to ride with continuity and to do well against the clock.

Planning the Jump Session

Following all this preparation you will want to do some pole work or actually jump some fences. This should be planned beforehand so that your apparatus is set up. It is pointless to warm up the horse and then get off him to put up the fences!

The fitness of your horse will determine the length of your session, but do beware of overtiring a young horse; if you go on and on jumping he will soon get fed up and may start refusing. Older horses, too, may become just as fed up or bored if they are made to go over and over the same fence. Thus we must discipline our own enthusiasm: we may love to jump, but it is important to remember that it is the horse which is doing all the hard work and he deserves consideration.

GYMNASTIC JUMPING

Many people ride for fun rather than for any serious reason. Although I can certainly go along with this in some ways, in my opinion the horse should also enjoy his work, which he will not do unless he is trained. I think that one of the most upsetting sights is to see a horse distressed, either from lack of understanding of his rider's wishes or because he is being asked to do more than his condition or level of training permits. It is up to each of us to make sure that this does not happen.

The Importance of Communication

When giving the aids during jumping there are going to be moments when there is some urgency either to lengthen or shorten the stride or to turn sharply. If you have developed the right rapport, then these moments should not emerge as a shock to the horse nor to yourself as your anticipation of likely events will have forewarned you of an outcome. Only experience will teach you such things, but unless you work hard to develop a sound communication system you could be in trouble.

Of course, positive thought and action is also necessary to success, and this often means gritting your teeth and riding hard. In this circumstance the rapport you have built up and the discipline you have demanded from your horse should see you through, but it is important not to get carried away and end up being thoughtless or rough.

Courses

Learning to jump a course does not necessarily involve going out and actually jumping courses, at least to start with. First of all you must be able to ride the route efficiently on the flat. It is a good idea to build the course you want to jump but then to ride around it, giving you time to decide exactly where you want to go. You can picture where you would take off and adjust the horse's stride accordingly. Imagine landing and what you would do, and whether you would want to ride straight or have a bend in order to present the horse well for the next approach. Think how much impulsion you would need for each fence and where you would push on, or check. Also exactly where you would ask the horse to change legs.

In this way you can train yourself to think ahead and plan precisely what you are going to do. If you programme yourself to do this, the actual riding of the fences can literally be taken in your stride.

Of course there are always unexpected incidents, such as getting a little too close or standing off too far and becoming unseated so that you are not in a strong position for the next fence. However, learning to recover is all part of the job. It is only made easier by developing a secure position in the first place and by training the horse as well as you can.

Falling Off

Sometimes even the best riders fall off, and you may or may not be one of those people who believes in holding on to the reins. Personally I used to prefer to roll clear if possible, but of course if you do the horse will probably run off and you could be ages catching it! The most important thing about falling off when you are learning is to get back on again so that you and the horse are united and can regain confidence together. Young horses are often especially frightened by their riders falling off and it can take some time to build up their confidence again.

Judging Speed and Energy

One of the most important things to develop is your power to assess the speed at which to ride into a fence and the degree of energy needed to get over it. If you go too fast the horse may get onto his forehand and be unable to project himself sufficiently upwards to clear the fence. Go too slowly and you risk the chance of a refusal, either because the horse has too much time to choose what he wants to do, or simply because there is not enough energy to get him over the obstacle.

Also there is the question of the going to be taken into consideration. At speed there may be more likelihood of slipping, but equally, if you do not push on, the horse may decide not to jump. Practice is the answer to most things, and only by constantly jumping a variety of fences will you learn to feel what is needed.

CHAPTER 12
Destinations and Objectives

There are many possibilities in horse sports: some owners will prefer to show in hand, others will wish to ride in one sphere or another. In this chapter I have set out some of the possibilities, with suggestions as to how the owner/rider may best reach his or her chosen objective. The following plan may help the reader to get his thoughts in order; and if it is applied it will also help him to get where he wants to go!

1. First choose the destination or goal.
2. Plan the route carefully.
3. Allow sufficient time to get there.
4. Be prepared for diversions or problems.
5. If the way is lost ask someone for help!

Some people find it easy to choose which discipline they want to follow. They may have known since childhood, and experience has simply reinforced their desire. Others find specializing a problem and may need to 'play' at various aspects of riding before eventually being able to choose. Of course quite often the whole matter is decided for you due to the size of your pocket or because the horse you already own is only suitable for one thing.

If you do have a particular ambition you may need to harden your heart and part with a horse which is unsuitable for one that is able to do what you want, because although good training can make up for many deficiencies, it cannot overcome physical limitations. If you do not wish to specialize, then the whole question of whether your horse is suitable is made much easier, because most horses can cope with different spheres of equestrianism if not required to reach great heights.

Next you must choose how you will reach your goal, whatever it may be; some people revel in a hazardous route, others prefer it plain and straightforward, and there are always different ways to get to the same point. For most people and their horses a steady, step-by-step climb is the safest way. The work involved is not always exciting but if you can be thrilled by small improvements and look upon the next step as a challenge, then training becomes an absorbing experience.

Quite often during training depression sets in, as work you thought you had established suddenly seems to disintegrate. This can be hard to understand, especially if you believe the horse's memory to be infallible once he has been taught a particular exercise. I think everyone gets downhearted sometimes, particularly as recapturing what you had can be equally hard. At these times it is a good idea to consider your progress so far, to go over the work in your mind and try to pinpoint where it began to go wrong.

DESTINATIONS AND OBJECTIVES

Nearly always you have to go back to basics – but then, getting over or around problems is all part of training, and you must accept the fact or give up!

Many of the problems that occur in training are because we are in too much of a hurry. We are anxious to progress, and perhaps we see others who started after us getting there more quickly. The sphere we have chosen may demand maturity at an early age, such as in showing. Unfortunately whatever the age, make or shape of the animal in question, only a daily routine of work will get you to where you want to go, and many of the problems that crop up are the result of impatience. It can be most frustrating to take more time to achieve a particular objective but at the end of the day it may be the best course of action.

When things do seem to have gone irretrievably wrong, try not to become too agitated as this will only make matters worse. If you absolutely cannot work out a solution to your difficulty you may have to go to the professional who, hopefully, will set you back on the right path.

Competing: Some Practical Considerations

If you are ambitious and want to compete, the following practical considerations must be taken into account: how to arrive at a competition in the right frame of mind, and how to overcome your nerves on the day.

Teaching yourself to drive your horse safely is all part of the job, but it is most important to the horse that he has a smooth journey and arrives calm and confident. Those who drive a trailer must anticipate a slower trip than those who travel in a lorry: a trailer tends to swing, particularly on major roads and motorways when it may be considerably affected by the slipstream of passing lorries. A lorry is altogether more stable, and providing the horse is not positioned so he is standing straight across, he will more than likely travel quietly. Do remember that pulling away quickly, stopping suddenly or swinging round corners will certainly be unbalancing for him; many horses have been put off travelling for life because of insensitive driving.

At the competition your horse may well lack confidence, and be unsettled by strange surroundings. You, too, may be feeling apprehensive, and your horse will know this. Probably neither of you will be able to work to the level you do at home, and this may be disappointing, but plenty of experience will provide greater confidence.

It isn't easy to talk yourself out of feeling nervous, but if you can really focus on the job you have to do, giving your horse your full attention, this will certainly help. Sometimes our horses do let us down by being unruly or forgetting their work because of the many distractions, but on the whole these problems can be overcome if the training and preparation is sound and thorough.

Showing

Hack Classes

The classifications are as follows:
a) Mares or geldings 14.4hh but not exceeding 15hh.
b) Mares or geldings exceeding 15hh but not exceeding 15.3hh.
c) Ladies side-saddle exceeding

DESTINATIONS AND OBJECTIVES

d) 14.2hh but not exceeding 15.3hh.
Novice mares or geldings which have not won a certain amount of money as specified by the British Show Hack, Cob and Riding Horse Association.

Apart from the novice class, horses should be dressed in double bridle and a show saddle.

Type

Horses will need good conformation and be able to move straight. They should show activity of the hind legs but not have a rounded knee action in front. In appearance they should have a great deal of quality with a suitable amount of bone for the substance of the body. A hack should not be in any way weedy, nor should it have excessively long cannon bones, be tied in below the knee, or be back at the knee. It should have excellent manners, be a comfortable and pleasant ride, and it should go well for the judge. Horses must be four years old or over.

Training

At home, training should proceed as for any other discipline, because the fundamental principles apply. How far a rider takes his training is up to him but a hack may be required to perform half-pass or flying change, and to rein back. It will need to show a good walk, extended trot and collected canter.

Riders will need to plan out and practise their individual show; this will probably be based on a figure of eight. To have a clear picture of what is needed it is a good idea to go to one of the top shows to see what the experts do.

As manners are so important, training in company will be essential. Start with a couple of willing friends who live nearby; their horses do not necessarily have to be hacks! Go out into a suitable paddock and ride round one behind the other, not too far apart as this might cause a novice horse to become over-excited. Space out gradually and practise riding past each other. Give each other plenty of space, and do this in trot and canter on both reins until the horses are going sensibly. This may need to be worked on several times before a horse is ready to go to his first show.

Standing in line must also be practised, as a show horse should stand calmly in response to only a light rein contact. He must learn to be patient and to wait his turn when it comes to giving the individual shows. Do not, however, go to sleep completely when in line, or allow the horse to do so! Although he should not be restless he should still be alert, and stand properly without, for example, resting a leg.

When it is your turn, ride straight forwards and stand the horse where the judge can see him properly; then when told, ride on forwards before starting your individual show. This should be fitted tidily into the space available where the judge can see it. Do not ride too close to the judge, or disappear behind the line up where you cannot be seen. At the end of your show the horse should stand still with the reins quite slack.

In training the horse should have been taught to carry itself so that it is light to ride. There is nothing worse to look at or to ride than one that leans on the rider's hands or has to be kicked along. When the ride judge mounts the horse must stand absolutely still. He or she may wish to have a leg up, but in any event any adjustment to the stirrup length should be made beforehand. The judge will want to ride a horse that responds to the aids easily and does not cause him or her any anxiety. A horse that is stiff or jarring will be uncomfortable, and will obviously not be looked on favourably.

When the time comes to strip the horse it is a great advantage to have someone reliable who will come in to help; his task will be to remove any sweat caused by the saddle and to tidy the horse generally. The horse must lead willingly with the rider by its left shoulder. The reins may be held together by the right hand about six inches below the bits, with the end of the reins and a riding cane held in the left hand. The rider must allow and encourage the horse to walk and trot freely, and not restrict it by holding its head tightly; he should turn it away from him at the end of his trot-up. Also never alarm the judge by going too close, although be sure that he can see that the horse moves straight. When standing the horse up for the judge, position it with one leg slightly in advance of the other in front and behind so that all its legs may be seen, and encourage it to hold its head in an attractive position.

Riding Horse Classes

These very popular classes are staged in two sections: up to 15.2hh, and 15.2hh and over. A riding horse should have a great deal of quality; in definition it is somewhere between a hack and a lightweight hunter.

The training of the hack would be applicable.

Cob Classes

A show cob is a cross-bred animal really of chance breeding. The classification is not

A young person turned out correctly for a show class.

exceeding 15.1hh, lightweights capable of carrying up to 89kg (14 stone), and heavyweights over 89kg.

Type
Although these animals must clearly be up to weight they must also have quality. There should be no suspicion of loaded, straight shoulders or tubular bodies, and the limbs should display short cannon bones, good flat bone and clean strong hocks. It is not too much frowned upon if they move with some knee action, but they must be able to gallop.

Training
When showing, the gallop should be a controlled build-up of speed with the horse remaining balanced and returning to a slower speed calmly without fighting the rider.

Quarter marks are an attractive addition to good turnout.

A good-looking cob giving a balanced ride.

Otherwise their training would basically be the same as for any other show horse.

Hunter Classes

The National Light Horse Breeding Society classifies the categories as follows:

- Lightweights: to be capable of carrying 80kg (12 stone 7lb).
- Middleweights: to be capable of carrying over 80kg (12 stone 7lb) up to 89kg (14 stone).
- Heavyweights: to be capable of carrying 89kg (14 stone) and over.
- Novice classes: the limitation depends on specified prize money won.

DESTINATIONS AND OBJECTIVES

- Ladies hunter: no weight classification; often ridden side-saddle.
- Small hunter: must not exceed 15.2hh, no weight limit.
- Working hunter: to exceed 15.1hh. There will be at least eight and at most twelve fences to jump, not to exceed 114cm (3ft 9in) in height.

It is often difficult to assess which category a horse may fit into. The amount of bone a horse has can be a guide, for example lightweights, not less than 20.3cm (8in); middleweights not less than 21.5cm (8½in) or so; heavyweights not less than 22.8cm (9in) or more. The height should be approximately 16hh for lightweights; 16 to 16.2hh for middleweights; and 16.2hh or over for heavies.

All horses must be four years old or over.

Type
Correct conformation is of paramount importance, as is moving straight. An active hind leg and slightly rounded foreleg action is desirable, with a good, workmanlike, ground-covering stride. Any restriction of shoulder movement or lack of balance is undesirable.

Because the hunter was originally required for going across country he should have a bold outlook, strong limbs and plenty of stamina, and these qualities are assessed together with his build, performance and ride.

Training
Many hunters seen in the show ring are allowed to go on their forehand, and this is unattractive and inhibits the freedom of the shoulders. Often, too, their riders insist on pulling their heads to the outside instead of riding them straight, which is unbalancing for them and gives them no chance to show their neck and shoulders to best advantage. They should be taught the correct principles if they are to be a pleasant and obedient ride.

Side-Saddle Classes

I am glad to say that riding side-saddle is now enjoying a considerable revival, and there are more showing classes than ever. In fact it is generally associated with showing, so as far as the horse is concerned good conformation would be essential if this is your aim. Most horses will carry a side-saddle if it is introduced sensibly, although some may not care for the balancing strap, and they may not like the feel of the habit, either.

Obviously it is necessary to train the horse to accept slightly different aids, the whip having to replace the rider's right leg. If you are patient, however, the new aids should present no problem once the horse understands. All dressage movements can be ridden side-saddle, which is quite a challenge to those of you who are interested!

Classes for Arabs

There are many classes in which Arabs can be shown, from in-hand classes to ridden ones. In pure Arab classes the animals shown are of pure Arab blood; in an Anglo-Arab class the Arab is crossed with a Thoroughbred. There is also a third category for part-bred Arabs, which are animals whose pedigree contains not less than 12½ per cent of Arab blood.

Type
Arabs should have correct conformation, just as any other horse, and although they

DESTINATIONS AND OBJECTIVES

A well-made Arabian being shown in-hand.

have certain distinctive features such as a dished face and a high tail carriage, such things as cow hocks or a weak back end – even though frequently seen – are not acceptable and are classed as faults as they would be in any breed.

Training
Many Arab horse owners explain their horse's bad behaviour as being the Arab temperament. This is a feeble excuse, because an Arab's only problem is that it is highly intelligent, often more so than its owner! They should be trained in exactly the same way as any other horse.

The Arab's floating action can be very attractive and a great advantage in showing and in dressage if controlled in the right way. Both pure and part-bred Arabs also jump well if taught properly; some are very bold and have considerable scope. These animals also possess a great deal of stamina and some are exceedingly fast; over the past few years they have excelled in endurance riding, and of course in Arab racing.

Other Varieties

Many people nowadays own spotted horses, palominos, American Quarter Horses, Morgans and others. All these animals have a society with which they can be registered. These societies provide breed standards, offer information and run shows so it is worth joining them. There are also societies for all the native breeds and these, too, are well worth joining if you have a pedigree animal.

Endurance Riding

Any horse can take part in endurance

DESTINATIONS AND OBJECTIVES

riding so long as the rider or owner is prepared to commit him or herself to a comprehensive fitness programme. This means training yourself as well as your horse, and being able to give the time to the necessary roadwork. Furthermore you might also bear in mind that unless you sit in the correct position and give the aids properly you will add extra burden to the horse, which already has enough to do coping with the distance and the terrain.

Also, thinness should not be confused with fitness. Although the horse will not have the stamina if he is carrying too much weight, he should certainly be hard and muscled, and not merely in poor condition. When preparing for endurance events do remember that both horse *and* rider need a progressive training routine, starting with one hour a day and building up to several more, depending on the distance you wish to ride.

Remember to give the horse plenty of energy-producing feed, reducing bulk as you near a competition.

As regards other training, every horse benefits from basic schooling: it helps him to work more easily and effectively and makes him a better ride. Also, a rider will be more in harmony with his horse if he learns to communicate in the accepted way, and if he understands the horse's need for consistent and sympathetic aids.

Team Chasing and Drag Hunting

Some of you will want to take part in these challenging and exhilarating pastimes. They have just as much to do with equitation as any other aspect of riding from the standpoint that all horses should be trained, and all riders should try to ride correctly in order to obtain good results. Time spent in a school is never wasted and can enhance a horse's performance in any sphere.

Those who want to take up this kind of cross-country riding will need bold, strong horses which must be fit and properly prepared for the fences they will meet. Conformation and type is relatively unimportant – but if you or the horse lack courage, do not become involved!

Horse Trials

If your aspirations lead you towards this sphere then you will need a horse which stands over 15hh. It will need to be strongly built, and able to gallop. It also needs to have a good walk, trot and canter for the dressage phase, and although it will need to be bold, its temperament must allow it to accept discipline. Thus small horses with a limited stride are going to be handicapped in horse trials: a horse which can gallop effortlessly over undulating ground is obviously more useful. Very big horses are also sometimes handicapped as they are not athletic enough, tending to get into trouble in trappy places. They are often late to mature.

A strong Thoroughbred or Thoroughbred cross is probably most suited to trials. His action should be free, but need not necessarily be straight.

Training

At novice level a fairly simple degree of training is required, with very basic movements asked for. However, by the time the horse is ready for Advanced competition he should be able to half-pass in trot and canter, counter-canter, do walk pirouettes, rein back, collect to a degree, and extend.

To begin with the horse may only be asked to jump fences at a height of 90 to 105cm (3ft to 3ft 6in); this increases as the horse upgrades, the fences being larger in width as well as in height.

Unless both rider and horse have the stamina, and unless the rider has the time to give to the training and getting himself and his horse fit, he should not contemplate this area of riding.

Show Jumping

Some riders may want to register with the British Show Jumping Association and jump affiliated courses; if so, there are plenty of graded competitions starting at a very novice level.

Almost any type of horse will do, *providing* it can jump to the level chosen, and this must be considered carefully; too many people with great ambitions have not made a good enough assessment of their horse's ability to start with. An expert may have to do this, as merely trying to jump over a high fence is not the answer; he will consider the horse's attitude when he is presented at a fence, and he will be able to gauge his scope from the way he tackles and negotiates the fence.

If it is decided that the horse has the required ability, his training should be carried on according to the basic principles of equitation. Moreover if he is to jump heights and be consistent, he must be fit and have sufficient muscle power, and this cannot be rushed: it should develop along with the gradual introduction of new fences and the use of gymnastic exercises.

Dressage

It may not be easy to know whether your long-term objective really *is* dressage, and furthermore whether the horse is suitable. Almost any animal can perform a simple dressage test, if trained; it is deciding upon the degree of proficiency that is perhaps the deciding factor. If the aim is the Olympic team, then both rider and horse do need to be gifted, the rider in sensitivity backed up by firm determination, the horse in scope and beauty together with the right temperament. Even at a lower level the rider would be deceiving himself if he thought he could be successful without hard work; and a horse must be able to show some considerable flair and talent in the paces if disappointment is to be avoided.

No one can say whether a horse successful in dressage competitions will be of a particular breed or height; almost everything is down to correct training and the will of the rider. It is certainly true that many who start out in dressage aiming at the top quickly become disillusioned because they have failed to grasp the real meaning of training. On the other hand there are riders who don't presume to aim at much at all, and find that their endeavours take them further than they could ever have anticipated.

Training horses is frustrating and fascinating: some provide unbelievable thrills, others break your heart! Whatever happens in the world of horses, for those who are bold enough to accept it, the challenge is there.

Index

accuracy, 100
action, 13, 19, 81
activity, 77, 87
aggression, 13
aids, 42, 48, 55, 56, 58, 61, 63
anticipation, 103
Arabs, 19, 140
arenas, 94, 95
assessment of horse, 7

balance, 77, 86, 87
bascule, 19, 126
boredom, 50
breastplate, 22, 67

canter, 74, 80, 127
cavaletti, 72, 126
cavesson, 67
chambon, 71
circles, 96, 97
clipping, 26, 27, 28
cobs, 138
collection, 108
communication, 61, 62, 133
combinations (fences), 128, 129
competitions, 39, 136
concentration, 40, 46, 101
conformation, 7, 86
contact, 61
cooling off, 50, 71, 120
counter canter, 113
cow hocks, 84
cross-country, 32, 129
curb bit, 21

discipline, 46, 64, 95
dishing, 13, 84
double bridle, 21
dressage, 18, 143
  saddle, 22

engagement, 87, 89, 106
endurance, 141
evasions, 90, 93
ewe neck, 8
extensions, 113

feel, 17, 45, 92, 101, 115
feet, 8, 9, 71
fitness, 45, 70, 119
flying changes, 113, 114

gallop, 81
general purpose saddle, 22
give and re-take the rein, 44
goals, 20, 135
grid, 128

hacking, 18, 32, 116, 118
hacks, 19, 136
half-halt, 87
half-pass, 90, 111
health, 25
highly strung, 9
hollow outline, 69
horse trials, 142
hunters, 19, 139

impulsion, 77, 87, 103, 134
indoor school, 31
instruction, 37

joints, 7
jumping, 19
  position, 131
jumps, 32

lateral work, 111
laziness, 9
leg-yield, 105
lengthening (gait), 70, 79
limbs, 7
livery, 35
long reining, 72
loops, 98
loose jumping, 129
loosening up, 48, 130
lungeing, rider, 45, 72
  horse, 67, 68

martingales, 66
memory, 45

nerves (rider), 39, 41, 51
nervousness (horse), 11, 12

obedience, 64
outline, 69, 83

pasterns, 9
physique, rider's, 16
  horse's, 48
pigeon toes, 13
pirouette in walk, 110

poles, 71, 72, 124
preparation for movement, 100, 132
problems (ridden), 102

rapport, 18
rein back, 111
renvers, 90
resistance, 91, 92, 109
reward, 42, 43
rhythm, 77
riding clubs, 20
  schools, 16, 37
road safety, 117
  work, 116
roller, 67
routine, 17, 50, 130
running reins, 66
schooling area, 29, 30
seat, 55
self-carriage, 89
sensitivity, 92
sequence of footfalls, 74
sequence of lesson, 48
serpentine, 98, 99
shoulder-in, 90, 106
showing, 19
show jumping, 19, 143
side reins, 69, 71
side saddle, 140
snaffle bits, 20, 21, 70
spurs, 65
straightness, 84, 86
stretching, 44
submission, 90
suppleness, 77, 89

tack, 20
temperament, 9, 83
trainers, 37, 38
transitions, 64, 78, 132
travers, 90
trot, 74, 79
turn on the forehand, 104
turns, 64, 99

variation of pace, 100
voice (use of), 43, 68

walk, 74, 78
whip, 64
wrong leg at canter, 103